Biblical Answers
to Your
Toughest Questions

Other Books by Walter Martin

Essential Christianity
(2022)

The Kingdom of the Cults Handbook
(Jill Martin Rische, co-author, 2019)

The Kingdom of the Occult
(Jill Martin Rische and Kurt Van Gorden, co-authors, 2008)

Through the Windows of Heaven: 100 Powerful Stories and Teachings from Walter Martin, the Original Bible Answer Man
(Jill Martin Rische, co-author, 1999)

The Christian and the Cults

Christian Science

Herbert W. Armstrong and the Worldwide Church of God

Jehovah of the Watchtower

Jehovah's Witnesses

The Maze of Mormonism

Mormonism

New Age Cults

The New Cults

The Riddle of Reincarnation

The Rise of the Cults

Screwtape Writes Again

Walter Martin Speaks Out on the Cults

Walter Martin's Cults Reference Bible

Biblical Answers
to Your
Toughest Questions

"The Bible Answer Man" Responds to Questions on the Trinity, End Times, Eternity, and Other Thorny Issues

WALTER MARTIN

Compiled and Edited by
JILL MARTIN RISCHE

CLC
PUBLICATIONS
Fort Washington, PA 19034

Biblical Answers to Your Toughest Questions

Published by CLC Publications

USA: P.O. Box 1449, Fort Washington, PA 19034
www.clcpublications.com

UK: Kingsway CLC Trust
Unit 5, Glendale Avenue, Sandycroft, Flintshire, CH5 2QP
www.equippingthechurch.com

Printed in the United States of America

ISBN-13 (paperback): 978-1-61958-384-9
ISBN-13 (e-book): 978-1-61958-385-6

Italics in Scripture quotations, if not in the text of the NASB, are the emphasis of the author.

Audio tapes by Walter Martin (mentioned in various places in this book) are available at www.waltermartin.com.

To my sweet sister, Elaine Martin,

for all her love and support.

"She opens her mouth with wisdom, and the
teaching of kindness is on her tongue."

(Proverbs 31:26)

Contents

Introduction

It's not common knowledge, but Walter Martin never named himself "The Bible Answer Man." This was a title given to him by his mentor and close friend, Dr. Donald Grey Barnhouse. The reason was simple: Walter Martin had an answer for almost everything.

He began with questions at a weekly Bible class in New York that finally expanded, in the end, to three hours of questions, five days a week, across America and around the world. For 35 years my father answered more questions than I'm sure he could ever count, and even though he is absent from the body and at home with the Lord, he's still answering questions today. This book is a sample of the many questions he answered down through the years—from Bible class to radio show—and I hope there will be many more to come.

My father liked to end on a song, and I will always see him singing this one in the front of the church, after a long night of answering questions:

> Blessed assurance, Jesus is mine;
> Oh, what a foretaste of glory divine!
> Heir of salvation, purchase of God,
> Born of His Spirit, washed in His blood.
>
> This is my story, this is my song,
> Praising my Savior all the day long.
> This is my story, this is my song,
> Praising my Savior all the day long.

Jill Martin Rische
March 29, 2023

1

The Triune God

Among the most common questions posed to Walter Martin were those having to do with the Trinity, the nature of the Godhead—Father, Son, and Holy Spirit—and His unique attributes. Here are Dr. Martin's responses to questions about these important areas of doctrine.

Q: *Please explain the Trinity.*

According to Christianity, the doctrine of the Trinity teaches that within the unity of the one Deity there are three separate Persons who are coequal in power, nature, and eternity. This teaching is derived from the clear teaching of Scripture, beginning in the first chapter of the first book. In Genesis, at the dawn of creation, an interesting conversation took place: "And God said, Let us make man in our image, after our likeness" (Gen. 1:26).

The significance of the plural "us" and "our" is no small issue. Either God was talking to Himself (a conjecture which even Jewish commentators reject), to the angels, or to other Persons deliberately unidentified. It's clear that He would not have been talking to angels because the next verse, referring to the creation of man, declares, "in the image of God created he him" (1:27). God never created man in the image of angels, but in the Divine image. In Genesis 1:26, the Father was addressing His Son and the Holy Spirit. No other explanation fits the context.

In Genesis 3:22, after Adam had sinned, God declared, "Man has become as one of us." Man recognized the difference between good and evil. Later, concerning the Tower of Babel, God said, "Let us go down and there confound their language" (Gen. 11:7). In both instances, the mysterious plurality again emerges.

The Old Testament prophets implied this same mysterious relationship within the Deity. In recounting his call to the prophetic office, Isaiah records that God asked, "Who will go for us?" (Isa. 6:8). Why didn't God say "me" instead of "us"? The answer is self-evident: God wished to testify of His threefold existence and nature.

The doctrine of the Trinity emerges from the New Testament Scriptures in several interesting places:

The Incarnation. The birth of the Lord Jesus Christ as described in the accounts in Matthew and Luke show that the doctrine of the Trinity was not a later invention of theologians. Luke records, "The angel answered and said unto her, The Holy Ghost shall come upon thee, and the power of the Highest shall overshadow thee: therefore also that holy thing which shall be born of thee shall be called the Son of God" (Luke 1:35). Since other passages of Scripture reveal that the term "Highest" refers to God the Father, we have in Luke a concrete instance of the Holy Spirit, the Father, and the Son all being mentioned together in the supernatural event of the Incarnation.

The Discourses of Christ. In John 14 and 15, Christ is telling His disciples about the preeminence of the nature of God and the unity of Triune composition. Jesus declared,

> And I will pray the Father, and he shall give you another Comforter, that he may abide with you forever; even the Spirit of truth; whom the world cannot receive, because it seeth him not, neither knoweth him: but ye know him; for he dwelleth with you, and shall be in you. (John 14:16–17)

Our Lord here prays to the Father for the Spirit, and His awareness of Triunity is quite apparent. In John 14:26 and 15:26,

Christ uses the same formula, mentioning the three Persons of the Deity and indicating their unity, not only of purpose and will, but of basic nature.

The Resurrection of Christ. A final instance of Trinitarian emphasis is that of the Resurrection of our Lord. In John 2:19 Christ declared to the Jews, "Destroy this temple and in three days I will raise it up again." John hastens to tell us that Jesus was speaking of the Resurrection of His earthly body (2:21). Other scriptures state that Christ was raised by the agency of the Holy Spirit (Rom. 8:11), and Peter states that the Father raised the Son (Acts 3:26), so again God's Word affirms the Triune existence.

Q: *What is Modalism? Could you explain that more fully?*

Modalism is an ancient church error of the third century. It taught that in the doctrine of the Trinity there is only one person, the Father. He appears sometimes as the Son, and sometimes as the Holy Spirit, which are only masks He hides behind, but at all times there is only one person and that person is the Father. He has modes of existence as the Son, and modes or projections as the Spirit, but He is only one person. That is modalism.

The New Testament is not modalistic. The New Testament is Triune. It teaches that there are three Persons—whatever "person" may mean—we have a hard enough time figuring out what person means on earth. When we start trying to figure out what it means in heaven, we're in real trouble. But there are three Persons: the Father, the Son, and the Holy Spirit, and the three Persons are all called God. This is the Christian doctrine of the Trinity: Three Persons, one God.

The Attributes of God

Q: *Can you define the biblical doctrine of the grace of God?*

The biblical doctrine of grace has been accurately defined as "the unmerited favor of God." The New Testament faithfully expresses the divine will when it declares that, "For by grace are ye saved through faith; and that not by yourselves: it is the gift of God: Not of works, lest any man should boast" (Eph. 2:8–9).

The sovereign grace of God—and it is sovereign or irresistible because mankind is its recipient wholly apart from merit—is the agency by which men are finally redeemed. Grace is fully manifested in the form of faith or more properly, "Repentance toward God and faith toward our Lord Jesus Christ" (Acts 20:21).

The New Testament reminds us that God justifies men only through His grace expressed in mercy (Titus 3:5), sacrifice (Rom. 5:9), faith (5:1), and finally, works (James 2:24).

According to Scripture, it is solely by grace that God shows mercy to a race deserving eternal judgment for the rejection of his Son. This benevolent mercy, in turn, produces faith in men who will believe in the atoning sacrifice of his Son for their sins, and as a result it produces good works indicative of true repentance, or proves repentance by deeds (Acts 26:20; Eph. 2:10).

So there is no confusion at this point, let us clearly grasp the fact that so-called "good works" can never save or justify the soul before God. In his Epistle to Titus, Paul declares that salvation is not the result of any "works of righteousness which we have done" (3:5), and in Galatians he reinforces this by stating, "But that no man is justified by the law in the sight of God, it is evident: for, The just shall live by faith" (Gal. 3:11).

Q: *Please explain Exodus 33:18–20 (where Moses asks to see God's glory).*

In the Old Testament, when God was taking the Jews through the wilderness after their escape from Egypt, Moses honored and praised God for all the miracles that were done. He gave God all the glory. Moses knew the Lord intimately: He knew Him in the burning bush and he knew Him by revelation. But still, he wanted even more intimacy.

As Moses is talking with God, God tells him that He is pleased with what he's been doing—he's been doing God's will. Moses seizes upon this opportunity. It's very beautiful, almost like a child talking to a parent. And Moses asks God if He is pleased with him to "show me Your glory" (Exod. 33:18, NASB).

What did that mean in the relationship that Moses had with God? What Moses was asking for was to look upon God. In other words, he said, "I want to see you as you really are!" Now, you'd think that a creature talking that way to the infinite Creator would be an affront, but instead God is delighted with the dialogue. He answers, "Right! Tomorrow, come on up to the mountain and I will show you My glory! But you can't look at Me, because if you do, you are no more."

I was always intrigued by that. God said, "Come on up, but you don't know what you're asking for. You are asking for intimate comradery with deity. You are asking to look into the face of eternity. You are asking to behold all power, all knowledge, all wisdom. You are asking to look at the radiance of the glory of God's very nature!" And you just can't do that, because if He should ever let you see that in your present form, you would be no more, "for no man can see Me and live!" (33:20, NASB).

That's why in the New Testament, the revelation of God is so intimate for us. That's why Jesus said, "Have I been so long with you, and yet you have not come to know Me, Philip? He who has seen Me has seen the Father" (John 14:9). In other words, He was saying, "You are seeing all that God can safely reveal to you now, in the person of the Son." So, the Lord Jesus Christ is the very intimate glory of God. Hebrews 1:3 says, "The Son is the radiance of God's glory and the exact representation of his being, sustaining all things by his powerful Word" (NIV).

When we come to know the Lord Jesus as our Savior, we come to experience God in a more intimate way. Moses wanted a more intimate relationship. What Moses was denied, we have beheld—the Glory of God in the face of Jesus Christ!

Q: ***A former theology student claims God cannot be sovereign when we have free will. He said it is well documented in a systematic theology. He also said you're in disagreement with him.***

I certainly am. The sovereignty of God does not exclude the free choice of man; it takes it into account. Now, how God's sovereignty and our freedom works out, I don't know. Calvin didn't and neither did Arminius—so why bother to understand it? The Lord hasn't told us about it, so let's leave it in the area of faith and quit while we're ahead.

Q: ***If God is merciful and compassionate, why do believers get cancer? Why do good Christians get killed in car accidents?***

You must understand the sinfulness of sin. The sinfulness of sin gives you a world which is cursed by sin. Why do faithful servants of God get struck down on the left and on the right? Because we are all under the judgement of sin (see Rom. 3).

Don't call into question God's attributes of mercy and compassion. Call into question the mess that we made of the earth in which we live. When God created it, it wasn't intended to be this way. The beauty that's in the world was God's idea. The mess was ours. Now, when we look around and see a world cursed by sin and we see judgment in that world—concentration camps, holocausts— we blame God.

Why do these things take place? Because man has the freedom to sin and God has the freedom to deal with it when He chooses to do so. He dealt with sin once and for all on the cross of Jesus Christ.

You live in an imperfect world. You are aging. You are born aging. You can't restore a perfect world. You can't go back to Eden again. The process of disintegration is what the world is all about—the curse of sin. It's not an over-simplification. God says that.

So, yes, there are tragedies. Yes, there are children who die at an early age. Yes, there are people who die suddenly. Yes, there are all kinds of sufferings. But the important lesson to learn from it is this: We're making choices, we've made choices, and the world is the result of those choices. But now things are different; we can make choices for God and ask Him to deliver us from these things . . . and many times He does.

If you only knew the number of times you've been spared sickness. If you only knew the times your life has been spared. One time I sat down and tried to remember all the times I was close to death, as an unbeliever and as a believer. I looked back on it and I said to myself, "How great is the mercy and compassion of God that He could take care of me so many times when I was certain to be killed or to die."

You live in a cursed world, but if God were not intervening in it—you think you've got problems now? You think the world's got problems? If God did not intervene in the world, you'd see much more evil than you could possibly dream of right now. So be grateful for the small percentage of evil.

Don't ever look at and doubt the attributes of God, the character of God, or what God did and why God did it. Take a good long look in the mirror at the mess we made of it, then say, "I thank you

Lord, Sovereign of heaven and earth, that you have been merciful and gracious and kind, and we are still alive." It is very unsafe to debate the character and attributes of God in His presence.

Q: *If God foreknew a certain event and it did not occur, can we say that God foreknew that event?*

No event that God foreknows will fail to take place. The question is not in his foreknowing an event or in his ordaining an event. The question revolves around how God does things. What is the divine methodology? What is the modus operandi? No one knows that. No one knows how God knows something. No one knows what God does in reference to predestination, foreknowledge, and His decrees.

You are literally flying blind because you do not have the mind of God, here. All you know is that God knows from all eternity who is and is not going to be saved. He never tells you on what basis, He just says He knows.

God also says He knows absolutely there will be people in heaven—He doesn't tell us on what basis, He just says He knows it, and He also says there will be people in hell, and they are there because they have rejected His grace. That much we know.

But the rest of it is a divine dilemma that Calvin tried to solve and ended up with double predestination, and that Arminius tried to solve and ended up with the sovereignty of human will. Neither one is accurate, and I wish I knew the answer to it. I can tell you all the things that are wrong with the different theories but when you ask me to produce an answer, I can't produce one because I have insufficiency of data.

I'm being as honest as I can. Any theologian who tells you that he understands the decrees of God in reference to predestination, you can right at that moment write off in that area, because he doesn't. He can give you his theories. I can give you theories too, but those aren't answers.

Look, this much we know: God knows who's going to be saved and you don't know on what basis. God knows who's going to be lost and you do know it's going to be based on their rejection of his will. How he integrates his sovereignty and human freedom is never explained.

Jesus Christ

Q: ***How do we know that Jesus Christ is really God?***

If you ever wanted two verses which teach the deity of Jesus Christ, I think Titus 1:3–4 would suffice. Verse 3 states, "God our Savior" and verse 4 goes on to say, "God the Father and the Lord Jesus Christ, our Savior." Jesus Christ is designated Savior and God is designated Savior—the same word.

How can Christ be the Savior without, at the same time, sharing in the nature of God? The Bible says God is the Savior of all men, especially those that believe.

Q: ***Should we worship Jesus as a man or as the Spirit of God that created Him? Is our salvation only because of Jesus coming to earth?***

You are to worship Jesus Christ as the Word of God incarnate. "In the beginning was the Word, and the Word was with God, and the Word was God. The same was in the beginning with God. . . . And the Word was made flesh, and dwelt among us (and we beheld his glory, the glory as of the only begotten of the Father), full of grace and truth" (John 1:1–2, 14). Acts 4:12 tells us, "Neither is there salvation in any other: for there is none other name under heaven given among men, whereby we must be saved." Some people say that's very narrow. It is. Some people say it's very restricted. It is, but God said it and it is therefore to be obeyed.

Q: *Matthew speaks of the "Son of man," referring to Jesus. Mark speaks of the "Son of God," referring to Jesus. Why the different references to Jesus?*

Luke, as well as Matthew, speaks of Jesus as the *Son of man*; this frequently-used phrase is taken from Ezekiel, and identifies Christ with humanity. Jesus was true mankind—the Son of man. So whether Matthew uses it or Luke uses it, *Son of man* speaks of the humanity of Jesus Christ, as well as His divinity. Mark speaks of the Son of God, and so does John, so we will never forget that though He is truly a man, He is also truly God in human form. That's where you have both designations: *Son of man* and *Son of God*.[1]

Q: *Why did the angel refer to Jesus as "that holy thing"?*

It is simply a biblical phrase, and "that holy thing" (Luke 1:35), of course, is the Person of Christ, or the Lord Jesus Christ. That's just a literary way of expressing it.

Q: *The Jews are expecting the Messiah to come. Do they believe He will be God?*

No. They've got enough evidence for it in the Scriptures, but they don't believe it. The Jews never expected that Messiah would be the Son of God. He was just going to be a deliverer or someone who was going to get them out of their immediate trouble. They always forget their own Scriptures:

> For unto us a child is born, unto us a son is given: and the government shall be upon his shoulder: and his name shall be called Wonderful, Counsellor, The mighty God, The everlasting Father, The Prince of Peace.

---

1 Editor's note: Both of these phrases—*Son of man* and *Son of God*—are used in reference to Jesus in *all four* Gospels. The questioner is correct that Matthew uses *Son of man* most often (with Luke using it nearly as often); however, it is the Gospel of *John* that uses *Son of God* most often.

> Of the increase of his government and peace there shall be no end, upon the throne of David, and upon his kingdom, to order it, and to establish it with judgment and with justice from henceforth even forever. (Isa. 9:6–7)

Obviously someone is called God here. I laughed when I read the Jewish translation of these verses in one of their Bibles. It says, "he shall be called the wonderful counselor of the mighty God," they just inserted the word "of". It's not in the Hebrew at all—they just put it in. That is deliberate misrepresentation. It's an absolute outright lie. They are still lying, 1,900 years after the fact. Some people say that sounds anti-Semitic. No, that happens to be truthful. The Scripture says who Jesus is—the King of kings and Lord of lords.

I had an orthodox Rabbi say to me one time, "You keep talking about the Son of God, the Son of God, the Son of God! We don't have a Son of God in Jewish theology. We have Messiah, the deliverer." I asked him if the Bible said He was the Son of God, would he believe it? He said "If the God of the Old Testament said it, I believe the law and the prophets."

I pointed him to Proverbs 30:4, "Who has ascended into heaven and descended? Who has gathered the wind in His fists? Who has wrapped the waters in His garment? Who has established all the ends of the earth? What is His name or His Son's name? Surely you know!" (NASB). That's a great apologetic—it's a great answer.

I had the most marvelous conversation about Messiah with another Rabbi. Rabbi Kellerman and I prayed together. I didn't try to beat him over the head with the gospel but I really stuck it to him on Scripture. He told me, "You know more Scripture than the rabbis do on the Messiah." I said, "I have to—my eternal destiny depends on it and so does yours!"

I pointed him to Proverbs and argued that if that verse is true, there must be a Son of God. He finally said, "It says it. It is food for much thought."

The Word of God must be believed because God said it. We had a great time together. I don't think the man is far from the kingdom.

Q: *Why did the Pharisees object to Christ?*

The Pharisees objected to Christ because, among other things, He claimed true deity. In John 8:58 Christ unhesitatingly taught, "Before Abraham was, I am," and John stated that He "made himself equal with God" (John 5:18). When we note that the identical term used by Christ in John 8:58 was used by Jehovah in His discourse with Moses (Exod. 3:14), we see that not only did Jesus fully understand His identity, but His enemies also understood His claim, for they "took up stones to stone Him" (John 8:59).

The Jews stated clearly, "For a good work we stone thee not: but for blasphemy: and because that thou, being a man, makest thyself God" (10:33). This, then, was our Lord's claim—nothing short of eternal preexistence. Some persons wishing to reject this teaching point to John 9:9, where the term "I AM" also appears in the mouth of one who obviously was not deity, thus "proving" that Christ's usage was not significant. They ignore, however, the context of John 8:58 and its companion texts, John 18:5–6. After Christ declared that He was Jehovah (I AM), those who came to imprison Him fell to the ground until He permitted them to take Him. The context of John 8:58 and the Jews' taking up of stones to stone Him for blasphemy (8:59) positively establishes Christ's claim.

Q: *How do I refute the Jehovah's Witness belief that Jesus is Michael the Archangel?*

Take them to Jude 9 where it says that Michael the Archangel, when he debated with Satan over the body of Moses, did not dare bring against Satan a blasphemous judgment but said, "The Lord rebuke you." Michael couldn't rebuke the devil—he didn't have the power—but Jesus rebuked him when he was on the earth. Even a little lower than the angels, Jesus was still the Word of God made flesh, and He specifically repudiated and rebuked Satan. That's why Jesus is not Michael the Archangel. He is the Creator of Michael the Archangel.

Q: *Can you give me one proof of the resurrection of Jesus?*

Nothing can be proven outside the testimony of witnesses or your own eyewitness experience. You and I were not there when Jesus Christ came out of the tomb, but other people saw Him alive with infallible proof.

One of the greatest psychological proofs of the resurrection is this: the same people who ran like scared rabbits when they took Jesus captive and brought Him up for trial—these same people, three days later, took a 180-degree turn. They suddenly chose to risk exactly the same death their Master had experienced. Psychologically, that's incredible, unless something happened.

If you believe every effect has a cause, what was the cause of the effect—the change in those disciples? We're not talking theology now, just plain old horse sense. What could have changed them from cowards to conquerors? There is only one thing that accounts for it: They saw Him alive! When they saw Him alive after they knew He was dead, they knew He had been placed in the tomb, and they knew there was a watch on the tomb to prevent anyone from stealing the body. When they saw this, they knew the gospel was 100% true and they were willing to die for it—and they did.

You don't die for a crazy Jewish carpenter whose body was stuffed in some ignominious Palestinian graveyard—you wouldn't and I wouldn't—and those boys were smart Jewish boys and they weren't going to, either. Something changed them, and it was the fact that Jesus presented Himself to them: eyewitness testimony. One of the greatest of them all was John 20. Eyewitness testimony shook the foundations of all of their thinking. When Jesus appeared to them and they touched His wounds, they knew immediately He had to be the Son of God because He was alive with infallible proof.

What is infallible proof? Science says that if there is any such thing as infallible proof, it is the repetition of the same experiment. Jesus rose from the dead and Mary Magdalene encountered Him—experiment one. The women encountered Him—experiment two. The disciples encountered Him—experiment three. The Apostles encountered Him—experiment four. Five hundred people saw Him after the Resurrection—experiment five. Each one of these is the repetition of the same experiment. They all encountered the same phenomenon. What was it? He was alive! That's what changed the history of the world.

Q: *Did Jesus receive a glorified body just as we will?*

Yes, we're going to receive a body like unto his own glorified body. There's no doubt about that at all (Phil. 3:20–21).

Q: *Why didn't Mary recognize Him after the resurrection? Could it have been because he was so badly beaten?*

No, because in the resurrection He rose in an immortal body. It was a body of flesh and bone, which had been transformed from mortal to immortal, and the reason she didn't recognize Him was not because He was disfigured and battered. In the resurrection, He had been restored as an immortal man. But He had the wounds in His hands, His feet, and His side, and the marks around His brow from the crown of the thorns and all the suffering He went through. That's true, but He was not disfigured so badly that He couldn't be recognized. The answer to your question is found in Luke 24:15, "And it came to pass that while they were conversing and discussing, Jesus himself approached and began traveling with them but their eyes were prevented from recognizing him."

So, it was not that the body of Jesus was so disfigured that He couldn't be recognized. It was that their eyes were prevented from recognizing Him until He opened the Scripture to them and bolstered up their faith, and their hearts burned within them from conviction.

Q: *Do we know what Jesus looked like? Are the pictures the historical church has today accurate?*

There is no description in the New Testament of Jesus of Nazareth, and no description that is reliable in history. The only thing we have is Isaiah 53 that talks about the suffering servant of the Lord who was Messiah, and you don't have a great deal of material in there except that He was not a strikingly handsome man. He was a man of sorrows and acquainted with grief. It's pretty obvious that when people saw Him, there was nothing about Him that would have attracted them normally, as one would admire a handsome man.

Q: *Do you believe that God hears and answers our prayers whether we ask in the name of Jesus or not?*

The Bible tells you, and Christ tells you, "If you ask Me anything in My name, I will do it" (John 14:14). Of course, He obviously means you can't ask Him for the Taj Mahal on your front lawn tomorrow morning—in His name—and expect to get it. He talks about a rational relationship with God—one of faith in God's ultimate judgment, and the fact that you're going to trust the will of God. If God gave you everything you had the faith to claim, you would be in a horrible condition in your life. Believe me, there are all kinds of things we can believe God for and if we ever got them, I shudder to think what would happen to us. We have a carnal nature and we don't know how to handle all of the goodness of God. So, all I can say is that we should be trusting the Lord and letting the healing come from Christ on Christ's terms.

Q: ***About the birthplace of Christ: in Matthew 2:11 it says a house, and in Luke 2:16, it says a manger. These seem contradictory—have I missed something?***

No, you haven't missed anything. He was born in a manger. When the wise men came, it was to a house. So, if you get a parallel account of something in the New Testament, you put the different accounts together and you'll see the meaning. The Bible does not say that Jesus was born in a house—it says He was born in a manger. The wise men didn't find Him in a manger though. The Bible says they found Him in a house. So there is nothing contradictory.

Q: ***The Bible says that God laughs, so He must have a sense of humor. Can you point to a place where Jesus used humor in his ministry?***

God laughs. The Scripture says He laughs and that means that He has an enormously diverse sense of humor. Now, don't mistake me, I think when we get to the knowledge of the holy, we ought to be properly reverent, but our Lord was a man of sorrows who still had a biting sense of humor. You'll find some references to it as you get into the Scriptures, if you check it out carefully.

For instance, one of His greatest humorous statements had to do with the Pharisees. After a very lengthy theological discussion with them He said, "I don't understand you. You strain out the gnat and swallow the camel." People don't grasp that in our day, but they made wine, not grape juice—fermented wine. They put thin gauze over the top of the barrels where the wine was fermenting to keep the gnats out; little bugs, but sometimes they got in. So, they would use a narrower or thinner gauze and then they would pour the wine through it, and as the wine passed through, it strained out the gnats. Jesus said, "When you make wine, you strain out the gnats, right?" "Right" said the Pharisees. "Then you swallow the camel," says Jesus. A very biting sense of humor, namely, what hypocrites. In winemaking you're marvelous; in your spiritual lives, you're camel swallowers.

Q: *Do you feel that Jesus was ever tempted to fall in love?*

As if love was a temptation! Are you equating love with lust? You can't do that. Jesus Christ came into the world and lived a celibate life. He said for this end was I born; for this cause I came into the world. Not to get married, not to raise a family, not to live a normal life. Jesus Christ came into the world to be the Savior of lost men: first the Jews and then the Gentiles.

Jesus was not attracted as we are attracted. He was the last Adam, the Lord from heaven, and perfection can only be attracted by perfection. There wasn't a woman that breathed on the face of the earth that could have attracted Him, simply because perfection demands perfection. He was the last Adam, the Lord from heaven. He wouldn't take any of the soiled daughters of the seed of Adam or any of Eve's children. I think that will probably answer it faster than anything else.

Q: *Can you tell me where in the Bible it says what Jesus did for fun?*

Sure! John 2 tells us He went to a feast in Cana of Galilee, and while He was there He created the very best wine out of water so that everybody would have a good time. You may say He didn't really do that, but He really did! Some say it must have been unfermented wine—baloney! Read the text. It was not unfermented wine—I don't care what anyone tells you. I can read the Greek as well as they can. It has nothing to do with the word wine (*oínos*). It has to do with the context.

The keeper of the feast came to Jesus and said that most men set out the good wine first. Do you know why that is? It's because good wine is highly fermented and after you drink some of it, enough of it, your taste buds are dulled and can no longer tell if it's good wine or not. At that point, they bring out the lousy gut-rot wine and you don't know the difference, because you can't taste it. That's what the steward said, and then he told Jesus that He had saved the best wine till last. That means you've got the best stuff, the vintage wine, and that is highly commendable. You've been serving good wine the whole time.

Any student of Semitic history will tell you it was fermented wine. Now, don't go out of here and say Walter Martin said it's all right to go home and drink wine. I didn't say that. I said don't try and say Jesus didn't do it, because He did. The Scripture says all things are to be practiced in moderation, and if someone is offended by you drinking wine, don't you dare do it in front of them because you're going to hurt them, and the Scripture says do not do that.

Keep it to yourself, says the apostle. Do you know what the translation of that is? Shut your mouth about your private practices. That's between you and the Lord. Leave it there. Now doubtless I will be misquoted automatically, but I'm glad it's on tape and I'm not urging alcoholism.

2

The Bible

The questions posed in this chapter range from the nature of the Bible, to differences in translations, to how specific passages are to be interpreted. In all these topics, Dr. Martin's answers are founded in a confidence in the full authority of the Scriptures.

Q: *Please explain why the Bible is the Word of God.*

We are asserting that the Bible is a revelation from God—that it does not just illumine our thinking but reveals to our minds things which God knows and which we are incapable of learning apart from His communication with us. What we mean when we talk about the Bible as the Word of God is that it is a compilation of 66 books which span a period of more than 5,000 years, written by multiple authors, all of whom testify to the fact that they had an experience with a spiritual Being whom they described as "the Lord" or "the Eternal One."

Q: *Is context really important when we read the Bible?*

Yes, we go to the context to figure it out. The problem is that you must keep reading carefully whenever you think there is a conflict in the Scripture. You always want to keep one thing in your mind as a Christian: the Lord your God makes no mistakes. So, if there is any problem you run across, you can be sure the problem is either with you not reading the text properly, or possibly the translation of the text needs further interpretation. That is why we check back with the original text.

Q: *Are The Living Bible and Today's English Bible sound?*

The Living Bible is not a translation. It is a paraphrase, and incorrect in many places. I have not ever and do not now recommend it as a study Bible. I certainly would not start basing biblical theology on *The Living Bible*, because Ken Taylor can't read Greek or Hebrew; he put down how he thought it ought to read. That is simply not good enough when you're dealing with the Word of God.

Today's English Bible is translated by the American Bible Society and the gentleman who translated it is neo-orthodox in his theology. He does not believe in the inerrancy of the original documents of the Scriptures. *The New International Version* (1978) is good. *The New American Standard Bible* (1983) is good. There's quite a number of good ones. You don't have to be stuck with that one.

Q: *In Genesis 6:2, it reads, "The sons of God saw the daughters of men that they were fair; and they took them wives of all which they chose." Some believe the term "sons of God" in this passage refers to fallen angels who assumed human form in order to marry mortal women. What is your view of this passage?*

Theological rubbish. There isn't one single verse of Scripture that supports it. It's a theory, pure and simple.

Adam is called the son of God. Do you know that? The sons of Adam were called the sons of God. Therefore, it is a reference to Adam's progeny intermarrying. It is not talking about angels that came as spirits, assumed human bodies (including sex organs), and reproduced a race of giants. That is mythology—get as far away from it as you can go. You'll find it in the book, *Earth's Earliest Ages*, still in print, unfortunately.

Q: *In the New International Version of Daniel 3:25 it reads, "a son of the gods." In the King James Version it reads, "the son of God." Which translation is correct?*

I don't think either one is correct. If you read the Hebrew of Daniel 3:25, you find that it says, "the visage of one of them is like *a son of God*," meaning an angel or messenger. I think it was the Lord Jesus Christ, but the NIV is incorrect to say "a son of the gods." Just because the word for God is plural in Hebrew doesn't mean it must be translated as a plural. The Hebrew plural is often translated as a singular. Therefore, I would disagree with the NIV in context.

Q: *Some people say, "I've got to keep all these commandments today or I'm going to be in trouble with God!" But you're saying I don't need to keep all these commandments?*

From Romans 8 we can distill this great truth: God isn't going to judge us to eternal hell because He has made us all over again in Christ Jesus. He's going to judge the church, His body, differently than He judges the enemies of the truth. He's going to meet every need we have by giving us the power to manifest His fruits, and through that to walk with Him and have fellowship with each other.

God will free us from the carnality of Adam and our sins by making it possible for us, through love, to have God's righteousness and the righteousness of his law as an everyday part of our existence. So you don't need to worry, just thank God you won't have to get up in the morning and say, "I have to work to keep all these commandments." You can roll out of the sack in the morning, hopefully onto your knees and say, "I praise thee Father, Lord of heaven and earth, that you have loved me and because of this, I love you. Grant today that I may walk in love, that the spirit of life in Christ Jesus, God's law, may dominate me. Help me to love you this day with all my heart, soul, mind, and strength, and help me to love my neighbor as myself. Help me to love the church of Jesus Christ as you did. Amen."

If you make this prayer a part of your daily life, following what God says in Romans 8, you will learn the glorious truth that your righteousness doesn't depend on you. Your faithfulness doesn't depend on you. It depends on the One who makes it possible for us to be faithful and to walk with Him. Jesus Christ so loved us, that on the cross He identified with us personally. Through His spirit, He wants to see each of us identify with God and with each other so that we may be one as He is one.

Q: *What is the difference between storehouse tithing in Malachi 3 and tithing in the New Testament?*

Storehouse tithing refers to the passage in Scripture which urges the Jews to bring all of their tithes into the storehouse so that God will be able to bless them, and also that at the time of trouble and the time of famine that there will be provision. This was a "tenth part" of their wealth. Storehouse tithing was an Israelite practice enjoined by God.

Tithing from a New Testament perspective is taught in the Book of Hebrews, where we are supposed to pay tithes to the priest who is after the order of Melchizedek, who is the Lord Jesus Christ. The man, Melchizedek, was a great man of such stature in his time that even Abraham fell down at his feet and tithed ten percent to him. Melchizedek was better—he was more spiritual than Abraham. Hebrews 7:8–10 tells us that the priesthood of Aaron and Levi was in Abraham's body, and they bowed before Melchizedek along with Abraham.

No priest ever arose from the tribe of Judah until the priesthood was changed. When was the priesthood changed? When

Jesus was lifted up on Calvary, and He yielded His spirit. What happened to the veil of the temple when He died? It was torn from top to bottom—the Holiest of Holies, where only the Aaronic priest could go, was open. It signified that it was now possible for the believer to enter into the very presence of God. We are now in the age of grace and under a new priesthood.

Jesus Christ was not consecrated to the priesthood by the laying on of human hands. No one had to lay hands on Jesus and say He was consecrated to the priesthood because Jesus Christ was the priest of a new order—the order of Melchizedek—He was ordained in eternity by God and on earth by the Holy Spirit (Acts 10:38). He took up a new priesthood of Melchizedek. He is not made after the law of an earthly commandment—the flesh—but after the power of "endless life" (Heb. 7:16). The word appears only once in New Testament theology—it means imperishable, indestructible life. Jesus Christ is a priest after the order of Melchizedek because He rose from the dead and exists now in the presence of God—not passing His priesthood on as Aaron and Levi had to do. His is an untransferable priesthood (7:24). Jesus holds the keys to the Melchizedek priesthood and it belongs to Him, and to Him alone. Christ is the new High Priest for eternity.

All the Jews fell down and paid tribute to the man Melchizedek. Paul said that if you belong to Jesus Christ, you are Abraham's seed and heirs according to promise (Gal. 3:29). If you're going to claim the promises of Abraham, then you had better pay tithe with Abraham. If you're Abraham's child, and Abraham paid tithe to Melchizedek, we are to pay tithe to the priest after the order of Melchizedek and that is Jesus Christ, who exists imperishable and indestructible. We don't give him something because we feel like it, but because we owe him. This is New Testament theology.

Grace proceeds from love and love is the nature of God. Grace compels us to give because Jesus Christ is our great High

Priest and we owe the Priest after Melchizedek a debt of grace. We owe God everything.

There is a tithe of grace in the New Testament. Jesus said, "It is more blessed to give than to receive." This is because in giving, we receive. The question that the Christian has to face is what is my personal responsibility to God?

Q: *So are you saying I need to give more than 10 percent as a tithe?*

We are to serve the Lord with our whole being—our life, our health, our substance. We owe God everything. The Scripture says that the debt of grace is greater by infinity than the debt of law. We are saved by grace alone, through faith in Jesus Christ. There is a compulsion of grace and that compulsion of grace is not ten percent or thirty percent but 100 percent. You can never give Him enough because you have been redeemed from eternal destruction by the blood of Calvary. It cost God's grace that to save us and we have an obligation to Him. You owe Him everything—start with ten percent for openers, not because the law tells you, but because grace compels you.

Q: *In Matthew 13:33, Jesus gave the parable of the kingdom of heaven as "like unto leaven, which a woman took and hid in three measures of meal till the whole was leavened." How would you interpret that?*

This is a thorny question, since there are different views of what it means. I would highly recommend G. Campbell Morgan's, *The Parables and Metaphors of Our Lord* (New York: Fleming H. Revell, 1943) because he covers virtually every view on the subject. I will give you what I think it says.

The kingdom of heaven is like leaven. Leaven is something which penetrates or permeates an entire lump of dough, that makes it possible for the bread to rise. So it would apparently, in its simplest interpretation, be that the kingdom of heaven is a leavening agent of God in the world that causes the will of God to be accomplished and the kingdom of heaven to be established on earth. It's progressive and it leavens the entire thing.

Leaven, by the way, has sometimes been used to symbolize evil, but in this particular case it couldn't possibly mean that, because it is a reference to the kingdom of God.

Q: *What does it mean to be a "slave to sin" (Rom. 6:6)?*

Paul says you are not to permit sin to rule over you. You are not under the auspices of law, but under grace. Unfortunately, the moment you teach this doctrine someone will pop up and say, "Wow, if I've died with Jesus and risen with him in the newness of life, that means I can go out and really enjoy sin. The law can't touch me and the law can't condemn me!"

But Paul was ready for you jokers. He said, "What then? shall we sin because we are not under the law, but under grace? God forbid" (Rom. 6:15). The Scripture is telling us here that if we yield to sin, we become its servant; it dominates us, and only Christ can set us free.

Don't you know that whoever you yield yourself to obey, his servant you are? If you obey sin, then you'll reap death. If you obey God, you will reap righteousness and life.

"But God be thanked, that ye were the servants of sin, but ye have obeyed from the heart that form of doctrine which was delivered you. Being then made free from sin, ye became the servants of righteousness" (Rom. 6:17–18). Notice the past tense here—you were the servant to sin.

God wants the Christian, in the great conflict of life, to recognize that we have great resources, and the great resource we have is the fact that we do not need to yield to sin.

Q: *Second Corinthians 6:14 says, "Do not be bound together with unbelievers. For what partnership have righteousness and lawlessness, or what fellowship has light with darkness?" Does this strictly refer to marriage, and if a person will not accept that verse, is there another verse I may use?*

You have to understand that the context of the passage is talking about Christian relationships. It says do not be unequally yoked or bound up together with unbelievers. The principle in context here has to do with being mismatched in marriage. It also has to do with the underlying principle of Christians getting themselves bound up in relationships with unbelievers where there can be no agreement, and where there's going to be inevitable division and confusion.

In fact, Amos the prophet spelled it out long before Paul did when he said, "Can two walk together, except they be agreed?" (3:3). How are you going to get along with people who have such a basic disagreement with you—light versus darkness, good versus evil? Christians should not be mismatched with unbelievers. Christians should not be in business with unbelievers. Christians should not be involved with unbelievers in terms of relationships that are going to stress or compromise their Christian faith.

There's no partnership between righteousness and lawlessness, nor any fellowship between light and darkness; Christ has no agreement with Satan. "And what agreement hath the temple of God with idols? for ye are the temple of the living God; as God hath said, I will dwell in them, and walk in them; and I will be their God, and they shall be my people (2 Cor. 6:16).

You have to go on from there to see the application: "Wherefore come out from among them, and be ye separate, saith the Lord, and touch not the unclean thing; and I will receive you, And will be a Father unto you, and ye shall be my sons and daughters, saith the Lord Almighty" (6:17–18).

Q: *Is there any other verse I can use? I showed this to someone and they wouldn't buy that.*

First Corinthians 7 also emphasizes this concept when the apostle Paul talks about a believer who is married to an unbeliever. The context is idolatry in both passages—the temple of God, idols, and the relationship or boundaries with unbelievers.

There are two people that are married and one of them comes to Christ. What is the relationship of the believer to be to the unbeliever? According to Paul, you are not to send the unbeliever away. You are not to divorce the unbeliever. You are to be a witness to the unbeliever.

God has called us to walk and to be a testimony to unbelievers.

> But to the married I give instructions, not I but the Lord, that the wife should not leave her husband. But if she does leave her husband, remain unmarried or else be reconciled to her husband. The husband should not send his wife away. For the rest I say, not the Lord, if a brother or sister has a wife who is an unbeliever and she consents to live with him, let him not send her away. And a woman who has an unbelieving husband and he consents to live with her, let her not send her husband away. For the unbelieving husband is sanctified through his wife. The unbelieving wife is sanctified through her believing husband. Otherwise, your children are unclean, but now they are holy. (1 Cor. 7:10–14, NASB)

Obviously, the children are holy because they are children of a covenant named between God and the believing partner.

The Scripture says, "If the unbelieving one leaves, let him leave; the brother or sister is not under bondage in such cases, but God has called us to peace" (7:15, NASB). In other words, we are to let them leave if they want to leave, but we are to specifically try to be reconciled with them and bring them to Christ. Now it also goes on to say that a person is free to marry if a relationship occurs where there is a divorce, but only in the Lord, which means that marriage for the believer is only in the Lord. Therefore, the believer cannot marry the unbeliever.

Q: *Could you explain Matthew 5:40, "And if anyone wants to sue you and take your shirt, let him have your coat also."*

What He's talking about here is the Christian being nonresistant to the forces of evil as a general testimony. Now, He doesn't mean that you don't ever resist evil. He means that you should have a good testimony before the world.

> Let your yes be yes and your no, no. Anything else beyond this is evil or from the evil one. You have heard this said, "An eye for an eye and a tooth for a tooth, but I say to you do not resist him who is evil, but whoever slaps you on your right cheek, turn to him also the other. And if anyone wants to sue you and take your shirt, let him have your coat also. And whoever shall force you to go one mile, go with him two. Give to him who asks of you. Do not turn away from him who wants to borrow from you. (Matt. 5:38–42, NASB)

So, all he's talking about is the enunciation of the life of testimony to the world or to the unbeliever. He's saying go the second mile with them if they give you a hard time.

Q: *Then what should a Christian do if someone brings a lawsuit against them?*

The Christian is not to resist that, but simply to let the law take its course. The Christian can defend himself, but Jesus said if they sue you at law and they win your coat, be willing to give him your cloak also, which means that you show no malice toward them.

The Christian is permitted to defend himself, but if they should win in a suit against you, Christ said, be willing to give them your coat or your suit or whatever it is after they have won something else from you to show that you have no malice. By doing this, you're a good testimony.

Q: *Biblically, does God look at all sin as the same or is there such a thing as a "greater sin" (e.g., John 19:11)?*

There are degrees of sin, just as there are degrees of punishment. There are some who will be beaten, said Christ, with many stripes (Luke 12:47). That was an allusion to a greater punishment than others. So, obviously, if there are degrees of punishment, there must be degrees of guilt.

Q: *First Corinthians 6:17 says, "But the one who joins himself to the Lord is one spirit with him." How can we actually be one spirit with the Lord?*

There is spiritual union with God—a oneness with God. It's not saying that you become God or that your spirit becomes God's spirit, or his spirit becomes yours. The word one there has the basic meaning of unity or agreement. So, we are one or in unity with God—one spirit with him.

Perhaps I can illustrate it this way: the United States is suddenly attacked by an alien nation, and the American people rise in one spirit in union against these forces. It doesn't mean that we all become one person. It means that there is a sense of purpose and unity for specific goals, which in this instance would be defense.

Q: *Isaiah 53:5 says, "With his stripes we are healed." Is that primarily a spiritual healing as far as salvation goes or can we also get a physical healing from it?*

First of all, the context of Isaiah 53 is the atonement of Christ, the cross. It's talking about salvation coming to us, not healing for our bodies. It's talking about the salvation of the soul. By his stripes or by his suffering we have been healed is a reference to Christ's death for us on the cross and the redemption of our souls, so we can lay that to rest.

When you move over to Matthew 8, you have in Christ's earthly ministry the statement that there is a fulfillment of Isaiah 53 where it says that He bore our sorrows and carried our griefs. Now if you look at it very carefully, you will notice that this is the statement made about Christ's earthly ministry, not the cross. It is talking about the fact that Christ during His earthly ministry bore the diseases and sins of other people away by healing them. He identified with us and He healed us.

Matthew 8 is not teaching that Jesus took our diseases, it's talking about the fact that right there in his earthly ministry, before He went to the cross, He was already dealing with disease and He was doing it by healing. Mr. Price, Mr. Hagin, Mr. Copeland, and a group of others are all in the Pentecostal tradition trying to argue that you can claim healing for your body on the same basis that you claim healing for your soul. The Christian church has never taught it.

Q: ***Please explain Romans 8:4–8: "That the righteousness of the law might be fulfilled in us, who walk not after the flesh, but after the Spirit. For they that are after the flesh do mind the things of the flesh; but they that are after the Spirit the things of the Spirit. For to be carnally minded is death; but to be spiritually minded is life and peace. Because the carnal mind is enmity against God: for it is not subject to the law of God, neither indeed can be. So then they that are in the flesh cannot please God."***

The Scripture tells us that there's a contrast between the carnal mind and the spiritual mind. But so often, when expositions are given on the carnal mind and the spiritual mind, you get to thinking that somehow, you're a schizophrenic, and that's not true.

Adam was created with specific mental as well as spiritual attributes. In the fall, those attributes as well as our bodies became subject to the law of sin and death. When we came to life in Jesus Christ, God gave us a whole new set of characteristics, a whole new set of attributes patterned after the spirit. From that moment on, our spiritual nature and what we inherited from Adam genetically, mentally, and physically, have been at war with each other right up to the present moment—and they will be that way until either Jesus Christ comes back again, or we enter his presence at the death of our bodies.

The apostle well knew this and so he set up these two tensions for us to learn something from it, and he begins with one of the most stupendous statements ever recorded in Holy Scripture: "There is therefore now no condemnation to them which are in Christ Jesus, who walk not after the flesh, but after the Spirit" (Rom. 8:1). The word condemnation is one you should write in the margin of your Bible. It comes from an old Greek word, which literally translates, "There is therefore now no judgment that ends in death." Isn't that beautiful? There is now no judgment that ends in death for those that are in Christ Jesus.

Q: ***Please explain Romans 3:11–12: "There is none that understandeth, there is none that seeketh after God. They are all gone out of the way, they are together become unprofitable; there is none that doeth good, no, not one."***

This reference comes from the Old Testament and is a description of the carnal nature of man in rebellion against God. All Paul is saying is "Listen, Jew and Gentile have the same problem. Nobody can stand righteous before God." He says to take a good look at the carnal nature of man. It hasn't changed from the old covenant. It was true then, it's true today, and it's true until we die and go to be with Christ or Christ comes back for us.

This is what we're really like on the gut level of our spirituality. We are all unprofitable; no one really does any good.

> Their throat is an open sepulchre; with their tongues they have used deceit; the poison of asps is under their lips: Whose mouth is full of cursing and bitterness: Their feet are swift to shed blood: Destruction and misery are in their ways: And the way of peace have they not known: There is no fear of God before their eyes. (Rom. 3:13–18)

This is carnal man. This is not the Christian. The Christian is dead to the law and alive by grace to the Lord Jesus Christ. If we find ourselves acting anything like this, the apostle says you know it's the flesh, you know it's the carnal nature. It is not after the Lord Jesus Christ—after the nature of God. That's all we're being told. That's what an unregenerate man is like, even though he would like to think of himself otherwise.

Q: *How could God cleanse us through Jesus—without the law—when He says He never changes (Mal. 3:6)?*

Jesus paid the price for our redemption. God never changed—He just implemented His eternal plan. He delivered us from the coming wrath and cleansed us by His Spirit. He implanted His Word in our very being, and He made it possible for us to actually fulfill the righteousness of divine law by faith.

The law was holy, righteous, just, and good. The perfect representation of the character of our heavenly Father, and when you and I came up against the perfect, we saw ourselves for what we were: lost sinners. The law revealed our sin. The law couldn't save us, but it could sure tell us we were lost, and that's exactly what it did.

But the righteousness of the law was a holy life. The law was telling us you're supposed to live this way. So that was the righteousness of God's law, to live in conformity to the will of God, and we couldn't do it.

The law was weak, operating through the flesh and it was obvious the flesh could not attain to the spirit. We stood, every one of us, condemned before God's law. The whole world stands condemned before God's law. We cannot attain to its righteousness, and we are condemned by its perfection.

The apostle, a great authority on law—theological law primarily—seizes that opportunity, and he says there is therefore now no judgment that will end in death for anyone that is in Christ Jesus. We're going to have judgment. We're all going to stand before the judgment seat of Christ. We're all going to give an account for the deeds done in the body. The Christian is going to be judged for what he or she did not do in accordance with God's Word and his will for our lives after we became Christians. The unbeliever is going to be judged on the works they performed and their lack of conversion. They did not accept God's Word.

There are many judgments mentioned in Scripture, but here's one that should delight the soul of every Christian. There is no judgment in God's economy, for anyone in Christ Jesus, that can ever end in spiritual death.

Let me tell you something—that's a nice warm feeling when you realize God said it. He said, "I'm not going to judge you to eternal death. There isn't that rule anymore for you. You are my children, my seed, a new creation in Christ Jesus. I will deal with you, but not as I will deal with those who will not believe."

Q: ***In Exodus 9 God sends the plagues on Egypt because Pharaoh refused to let the Hebrews go. In 9:2–3 it says if they refused to let them go that the hand of the Lord would bring a terrible plague on their livestock in the field, including horses, so of course all the livestock of the Egyptians died. So my question is, how could Pharaoh send out his horses and chariots later on in Chapter 14, if they were all dead in Chapter 9?***

This refers to a very severe pestilence on the Egyptian livestock that were in the field (Exod. 9:3). It is a reference to the productivity of the Egyptian fields. In other words, the plague came on the animals that were domesticated, that worked in the fields, and that actually served the needs of the people because the idea was to cut off their food supply. So, the plague came upon the livestock in the field. There's your key—the pestilence was calculated to destroy the productivity and the wealth of Egypt. The horses that were in the chariots, and every other animal that was not producing anything—what would have been the purpose in their dying?

Q: ***I read something that really puzzled me in Matthew 11:14: "If you are willing to accept it, he is Elijah who is to come."***

First of all, Luke 1:17 says that the child John would come in the spirit and power of Elijah, and that means he would be similar to Elijah. Secondly, John was asked, "Art thou Elias? . . . Art thou that prophet?" The answer was, "I am not" (John 1:21). So, we know right there that John has finished the argument. He's not Elijah.

Now we come to Christ's statement in Luke. The Jews believed that Elijah would come before the great and terrible day of the Lord, and he would turn the hearts of the people towards God. Christ, knowing full well the truth, says you're looking for Elijah the prophet literally. That's going to be at the time of the day of the Lord when I return in judgment upon the earth; that's not this time.

If you really want to look for Elijah, then you ought to look at John the Baptist, because John is Elijah, which means that John was fulfilling the ministry—the spirit and power of Elijah in calling the people to repentance. Jesus was not saying that John the Baptist was a reincarnation of Elijah. No, he was seen in the spirit and power of Elijah. He's talking here about John fulfilling the role of Elijah. Jesus is identifying John's ministry with the spirit and power of Elijah. That's all he did.

Q: *Revelation 17:1 refers to the great whore. Who is that?*

The great whore is a religio-economic and political organization that will be manifested at the end of the ages, and it will be a vehicle for human cooperation with the Antichrist. The argument generally goes that the European common market fulfills the borders of the old Roman Empire, and therefore the restoration of the Roman Empire is imminent in this organizational structure. The great whore that sits upon the waters is actually a religio-economic political combine that is going to preside over the earth at the time of the revelation of the Antichrist.

Now, there's a division of opinion as to who constitutes this authority. The reformers of the 14th and 15th centuries on up in Reformation theology believe that it was the papacy, and that Rome was the great whore that sat upon the waters—the accursed city that sits upon Seven Hills. That was the interpretation at that time. It has been carried on by some theologians right to the present.

There are others that say, no, it's not the papacy. It's not Rome. It may center in Rome, but it wouldn't be the papacy. That's another school of thought. My own personal feeling is that the outline is clear. It's a religio-economic and political power. Now I'm not prepared to go beyond that yet, though it could well be an apostate papacy in the end.

Q: *In Exodus 4:24, the Lord had just finished telling Moses to go see Pharaoh. In verse 24 it says that at a lodging place on the way, the Lord met Moses and was about to kill him. How does that verse fit with what's going on here?*

Moses had neglected the rite of circumcision for his own child, and that circumcision was the seal of God's approval of the Covenant. So, the Lord met him on the way and the translation of the text says that He "sought to kill him".

The meaning of the passage is pretty clear in context. The Lord was sitting in judgment on him and threatened him with execution if he did not obey. So Zipporah took a flint and cut off her son's foreskin, and threw it at Moses feet and said, "You are indeed a bridegroom of blood to me," which means you have not obeyed the Lord. Here you are trying to lead people out of Egypt, and here you are trying to be the servant of God, which you are supposed to be, and what are you doing? You're disobeying Him. You didn't even take care of your own son. She said you are "a bridegroom of blood" because of the circumcision that needed to be done. And God decided to let Moses alone.

Q: We read in the Bible that adultery is wrong, so why did God allow Jacob to have a child by Leah's maid, Zarephath when he was already married to Leah?

In the Old Testament, God permitted polygamy and He also permitted concubinage, so this relationship with both Leah's maid and Rachel's maid were under concubinage. God did not sanction it. He did not say he agreed with it. He did not endorse it. He did not recommend it, but He permitted it to take place for purposes known only to Him.

My suggestion would be that we understand that what God did was let man have multiple wives and multiple concubines for the purpose of teaching him that marriage didn't work that way. It wasn't intended to work that way. In the beginning God gave Adam, Eve. He did not give him Eve, Mary, and Samantha. He did it for a purpose.

One good woman is more than enough for one good man. All of those things were permitted to teach us that one man and one woman is God's ideal way. The more we read about polygamy in the Old Testament, the more we see that it was surrounded by unhappiness, jealousy, and many other dark things.

Q: *Who decided what scriptures were going to go into the New Testament? And when did the first actual New Testament come out?*

No one really sat down and decided what was going in and what was staying out. What happened was that the words of the Gospels of Matthew, Mark, Luke and John, the book of the Acts, the Epistles of St. Paul—all of these were well known in circulation in the first century of the Christian church.

We know that from the writings of the church fathers in the second century that the complete canon of Scripture, as we have it today, was already in circulation before the year 100 closed. The churches that received the Epistles—Ephesus, Galatia and Corinth—knew that they were genuine because they were sent by Paul and bore a signature, so they didn't have any problem with this. Those documents were kept and many copies of them were made.

Going into the second century, we have this great collection of material that was known to have originated with the apostles and the inspired writers of the Scripture. All of this material was accepted by Christians, pretty much universally.

Then, there was a lot of material that we call apocryphal material, pseudepigrapha material, material that was not canonical. It really didn't have any authority, and was considered "legend literature" that grew up in the latter part of the first century and into the second century. So, as this material all began to accumulate, it became necessary to use a standard—that was the Gospels, Acts, Paul's Epistles—the standard or Canon to measure other materials by.

They used this rule or the standard to measure the other materials—they put these other materials beside what they knew was inspired Scripture, and whatever didn't measure up to it was discarded. This was officially done in the year 364 at the Council of Carthage. A council of Christian leaders from all over the church came together, and they evaluated all of this material using this standard. It was voted upon and discarded.

You can find a thorough study of the inspiration and canonicity of Scripture in a book by R. Laird Harris called *The Inspiration and Canonicity of Scripture*.

Q: *Was the flood of Noah local or worldwide?*

The purpose of the flood as indicated in the Scriptures was to destroy human and animal life. I think that purpose was accomplished by the flood that took place as recorded in the Book of Genesis. Wherever man was—anywhere on the earth—he was destroyed.

Q: *Are some things in the Bible just symbolic?*

Yes, the Bible is filled with symbols, such as the fruit and the tree in Genesis 2 and 3. Scholars maintain this many centuries back to the church fathers. In fact, "the tree of knowledge of good and evil" was a symbol for choice in the Garden of Eden; choice between God and the devil. Others have said it was a literal tree. What you believe depends upon your theological persuasion. I always deal with it this way, whether their names were Adam and Eve or Mabel and Charlie, there were two people at a given point in time who represented the human race, and they were finitely perfect. They willed contrary to the will of God and they sinned, and we have been picking up the pieces of that sin ever since. So, I happen to believe that there was a literal fall. Now how it was managed could be debated by theologians for a long time.

Q: *How would you respond to the claim that the New American Standard has taken out 150 verses compared with the King James Version—even more than the New International Version?*

I would respond to it by saying that those making the criticisms are, generally, not scholars. That's number one. Number two, the best texts of the New Testament omit a lot of these passages or have condensations of them, so the scholars have taken the best readings and put them into the texts. You'd have to be a textual scholar to be able to understand how it works.

I've been over the material. Let me assure you that nothing is missing from the texts that the apostles intended to be there. You can be certain of it—it's all there, and there are 30,000 to 300,000 fragments of the New Testament in Latin, Greek, Aramaic, etc. If you want to put them all together and spend the rest of your life comparing each one verse by verse, good luck with that.

3

The Church

What is the church? How should it be structured? How do we deal with differences in denominations? Are some church traditions more valid than others? Dr. Martin takes on these and other issues by appealing to principles of Scripture.

Q: *When people fall under the power of God, is this scriptural? And where is it found?*

Do you mean when people fall down or claim to have been slain in the spirit? Is it genuine? There is evidence of people falling down under the power of God: Paul on the Damascus Road was knocked off his horse and fell to the ground. Another instance is when the apostle Peter is on the roof at the sixth hour, where he went to pray before lunch. He hadn't eaten, became weak, and fell down. The Scripture says he fell down in a trance or he was given a vision by God. Those are the only two references that I am aware of in the New Testament. I don't know whether you could call that falling under the power the way people talk about it today.

I used to think a lot of this was psychological until one day I was preaching in the main church auditorium and the spirit anointed me at a specific moment. I felt the presence of the Lord in a very unique way. It went all the way through me like an electric charge. I knew something was going to happen, and I really preached like fury on a specific subject, and the Spirit of God just breathed over the entire audience. In that moment, I did something I seldom ever do—I said to the people, "'Now is the accepted time . . . now is the day of salvation' (2 Cor. 6:2). Now is the time to receive Jesus Christ." The power of God was absolutely fantastic. I couldn't believe it. You see? That was the preaching of the gospel.

Then, I felt the power of the Holy Spirit move on me and He said, *Why don't you pray for people who are sick?* I said, "But I'm a teacher—I'm not a healing evangelist." The Lord said, *This morning you're a healing evangelist.* I said "Fine, I'll pray for the sick." The Holy Spirit said, "Do it." So, I walked over to the front row and asked if there was anyone sick. I couldn't believe I was saying it.

A few people pushed others aside and came forward. I started to lay hands on them and pray for them, and all of a sudden they were falling down on the ground as if someone hit them with a baseball bat. I knew it wasn't me. I knew it wasn't them because they were down and knocked out.

So here we were; I was giving God all these very intelligent equivocations, for what's going on, and the Holy Spirit said, *Put it to the test.*

I said, "Alright, how?" I have dialogues with the Holy Spirit all the time. This answer came about 20 seconds later and the room was filled with the power of God. I couldn't get to someone in the third row, so I held my hand out over the audience and as the arc of my hand went up across the audience, the people fell. It was incredible to watch. I couldn't believe I was seeing it.

I said to God, "That does it—you're really here," and I started praying for people. Later on, a lady came back to see me after the service. She said, "I didn't come forward for healing before. I came forward because I needed a job and I needed prayer."

I said, "Praise the Lord."

She said, "I was walking across the parking lot on my way out, and I suddenly realized I wasn't limping anymore. I had a disease in my foot and my leg, and I haven't been able to walk well for years but God did something. Even though I went forward just for a job, God decided to touch me."

Boom, her foot was healed.

She came back a few weeks later to confirm it, and guess what? God gave her the job, too.

God healed her foot, and I believe He wouldn't have done that unless He was going to give her a job. I know Him well enough to know He does things like that. So, you don't make fun of the power of God and you don't get suspicious of the power "falling" on people unless there's real evidence that someone is just whipping up an audience. There are people who do that. There are people that capitalize on your emotions—they try to get you to identify with a certain feeling. I'm not talking about that. I'm talking a genuine manifestation of the Spirit, and when that happens, you'll know it.

It's not going to be some guy trying to con you into coming up and falling down so you can get under the power. It's going to be God touching you at a specific moment. I believe it happens, but we should test it and not just accept it point blank because someone says so. There are a lot of phonies running around in the world who work their way into the church. Satan is never so successful as when he gets near the altar. He creeps in close to the things of God—that's when he tempts and tests. You've got to watch that very closely because you're vulnerable at that point.

Q: *Please explain healing services.*

Well, it's a healing service. They pray for the sick and people get healed. Now, God is sovereign. God heals people in accordance with His own will. You can't whip the Holy Spirit up, nor can you call Him down. What you can do is ask Him, and if you ask in accordance with His will, He will heal you.

Q: Does God always heal?

It is not taught anywhere in the Scriptures that God's will is to heal everyone all the time, just because they have faith. That is not in Scripture. Now, there are people who teach this, but they don't have any Scripture to back it up. There are lots of people who prayed to God in faith believing, and they are not healed at that moment. Be honest; you prayed to God, you really believed He could heal you, and you were trusting Him in that, but your Father said no. That doesn't mean He's mad at you. It doesn't mean you're a failure at faith or you're a second-class citizen. It means Daddy said no, for His purposes.

If you read John 9:2–3, you'll find the answer there. They said, "Who sinned, Master, this man or his parents that he's blind?" Jesus said, "Neither one of them, he's blind that the works of God may be seen in him." Sometimes the works of God are healing, and sometimes the works of God are seen in the example of suffering for Christ's sake.

There are godly people who have been afflicted and who suffer bodily, emotionally, and mentally for Jesus' sake. It is cruelty to tell them that the reason they're suffering is because they don't have enough faith. Who made you God the Holy Spirit that you know what is in the hearts of people?

Think about it—how can a crazy "evangelist" with a couple of Bible verses ripped out of context make demands and take authority? That's no authority. The authority for healing is the Word of God, and the power of the Holy Spirit.

I believe in divine healing. I pray for the sick and I have seen miracles, and God healed me. I know the power of God, and that's why I'm telling you right now, it is cruelty to tell people that they do not have enough faith for God to heal them. It is God who decides to heal—not us—and we must leave that choice with him.

Q: *A friend of mine is reluctant to share her faith because she does not feel that she has the personality to witness. Is personality necessary to be an effective witness? How can one become a confident witness?*

There's no substitute for experience. You begin—you just start talking. Find something in the conversation that will lead you to a spiritual illustration. Ask God to help you do it and it will feel almost as if the words just appear in your mouth, but you are not doing it. The Spirit of God gives the words to you.

A wonderful illustration of this is the day I was talking with Rocky Marciano, one of the greatest Heavyweight Champions of the world, at JFK airport in New York. We were talking about boxing, and before we arrived in Detroit, I discovered at least 20 illustrations of salvation in the stories he told me. He couldn't believe it!

How do you get God out of a boxing ring? It's easy—we've already been knocked out. The referee counted to 10 when Adam hit the deck. Right? God has to rewire our circuits and put us back on our feet. Oh, we had a marvelous time, and that was all about boxing.

My teacher, Donald Grey Barnhouse taught me that in order to be able to communicate, you must be able to illustrate. As we walked down the street—any street—he would point to something and say, "Give me an illustration from the Bible on that subject." I was terrified, but I learned how to illustrate, and one day I did it to him. I pointed to a fire hydrant and I said, "Illustrate."

He said, "Red is a color of danger. We are in danger, but red is also the color of blood. God has overcome danger by the blood of the cross." That blew my mind, so I set about automatically developing illustrations from every conceivable subject. You can do it too.

Sometime after that, I walked into a store in New Delhi, India. It was a weird place for preaching. The guy showed me rugs and other things, and I saw this beautiful rug—absolutely gorgeous. I'd been talking with the shopkeeper about it, and suddenly thought of an illustration.

I said, "Isn't it remarkable how man designs these things, and even more remarkable that the Creator designed us?" The man who ran the shop turned around in surprise and said, "I never thought of that before." I said, "Good," and then we began talking about Hinduism and Jesus Christ.

Forty minutes later he shook his head and said, "Who are you anyhow?" He entertained an "angel unaware" because an angel from the Greek means messenger, a messenger of the Lord. I was sent there to tell that man something, and you have to tell people. They may get mad, but you must tell them.

Q: *Our daughter's best friend is a Mormon, daughter of the state bishop. How do you share with a 13-year-old without driving her away or causing her parents to prohibit her from coming to our home?*

The way to reach a person in the cults is with the love of Christ—to demonstrate Christ to them by the way you live as well as by the way you speak. Don't attack the people who founded the cult, but contrast some of the teachings of the organization with what God says in His Word. If you eventually end up criticizing the founders, the person is more likely to accept that the criticism is on the basis of historical fact, and that you are not antagonistic to people.

This young girl desperately needs the Lord Jesus Christ, the real Jesus. In Mormonism, she does not have the real Jesus. She has many gods instead of one God, so a good place to start is the person of Jesus and what it means to have a one-on-one relationship with Jesus Christ. The Mormon church is repentance, baptism, faith, and good works. Jesus said that whoever accepted Him would be saved—He said nothing else was needed—only Him.

Be patient and loving, and demonstrate the fruit of the spirit. As you're talking, you keep praying that God will touch her mind and her soul, and open her eyes so she can see Christ. He can do it marvelously if we are willing to trust Him.

Q: ***The Church of Christ doesn't believe that you should use musical instruments in church. They say that instruments aren't mentioned in the New Testament and it's a sin to use them. They won't go by the Old Testament. What can we use as a defense?***

Stop wasting your time. "The kingdom of God is not meat and drink" (Rom. 14:17)—or music or dancing, for that matter! The kingdom of God is righteousness, joy, and peace in the Holy Spirit. The problem with the Church of Christ is they resist the Holy Spirit.

The Holy Spirit is doing things today and the Church of Christ is saying, "No, He isn't." But the truth is that yes, the Spirit is doing them. Don't argue about instruments in church. Who cares whether you have instruments in church or not!

The big issue is what about you in church? What are you doing after you leave church? What gospel are you preaching? Never mind the instruments. If you're looking for a verse in the Bible that says you can play music in church, forget it.

The Old Testament set the pattern: there was worship in church and there was music. What was good under the Old Testament covenant should be good under the New Testament covenant. There's no violation of anything God said, so why get stressed about it? They're stressed and we shouldn't be that way.

Q: ***What did Paul tell Titus when he sent him to Crete?***

Paul called Titus "my genuine son." The Greek word there is genuine, my genuine son after the common faith. "Grace, mercy, and peace, from God the Father and the Lord Jesus Christ our Saviour" (Titus 1:4).

He sent Titus to Crete after telling him that he was part of the elect, that he acknowledged the truth—which is after godliness—and that the Christian lives in hope of eternal life "that God, who cannot lie, promised before the world began" (Titus 1:2). The Greek says, "the non-lying God, who promised before the times eternal," and made it clear, through His Word, and through the preaching of God our Savior.

Q: *Is there a specific way a church should be set up?*

Paul says, "For this reason, I left you in Crete." Titus was told to set in order the things that are "wanting." He was told to ordain elders in every city as Paul instructed, and "to rebuke them sharply that they may be sound in the faith" (Titus 1:5, 13).

So, Titus was there to set the church in order. This was the beginning of his ministry, and it's also a pattern for how Christians should live in the midst of a hostile and evil age. Notice something else that's very important here: God placed a specific order in the church. That order has been violated by a large segment of the Christian world. One of the reasons why you have such confusion, division, schism, and absence of authority is because people ignore what God said, and how God did these things. Whether we like it or not, the record still tells us what God did.

I'd like you to take a good look for a moment at just exactly how this order was set up. In Ephesians 4:8, we have God telling us how the order was ordained. It says that God gave gifts (*domata* in the Greek). He gave some to be apostles, prophets, evangelists, pastors, and teachers. These gifts are not in a numbered, "1 to 5" type of order. It is Paul simply enumerating what God has done in the church—the apostles and the prophets were given.

That's the foundation because in Ephesians 2:20 we are told, "You have been built upon the foundation of the apostles and the prophets." You weren't built upon the teachers. You weren't built upon the pastors. You weren't built upon the evangelists. You were built upon the foundation of the apostles and the prophets, with Jesus Christ as the chief cornerstone.

Q: *Please explain what Jesus meant when He said, "On this rock I will build my church" (Matt. 16:18).*

Peter gives us a beautiful picture in First Peter 2 of the building of the church. He says that we are all small stones or bricks built up into a spiritual tabernacle or temple. Jesus Christ is the chief cornerstone of the whole thing, not Peter.

Peter did not interpret Christ's words in Matthew 16 to mean that he was the foundation of the church, because in First Peter 2 he denies it and points to Christ as the foundation of the church. He is the stone laid in Zion and whoever believes in Him will not be ashamed. It is not me, says Peter, but Jesus.

Everyone is a small stone, a little brick built up into a great spiritual temple, but Christ is the cornerstone. You are built on the foundation: Jesus Christ, the apostles, and the prophets. Everything else rises from that.

That is the foundation that was laid forever: apostles, prophets, and then Jesus Christ as the cornerstone of everything. You and I are just little bricks in God's spiritual temple. We are all resting upon the authority of the apostles and the prophets, and Jesus Christ the cornerstone. All of this is going to be until the unity of the faith and the knowledge of the Son of God is attained to complete man unto the measure of the stature of the fullness of Christ.

Q: *Where does First Corinthians 12 fit into the divine order of the church?*

If you really want the divine order, you've got to go to First Corinthians 12 where the order is set up. God has set in the church first apostles; second, prophets; and third, teachers. After that, everything else of the gifts of the Holy Spirit follow: miracles, healing, tongues. All the rest follows the divine order of authority. You must have apostolic order.

Q: *Paul mentioned weaknesses in the early church—can you explain?*

Notice in First Corinthians (12:28) that after apostles and after prophets comes what? Teachers. What is a teacher? Somebody who knows more than you do. If the person didn't know more than you, then you would be the teacher. One of the great weaknesses in the church, and Titus ran right into it, was that the new converts thought they knew more than the leaders!

They had an ecstatic experience with Jesus Christ. They're filled with the Holy Spirit. They're climbing out on cloud 11 with this glorious manifestation of what God was doing. Sound familiar? So Paul says to Titus, "Now when you get there, for heaven's sake—and I mean it literally—do what I told you to do. I want you to set up the chain of command or authority in the church because if you don't do it, the implication is you are not going to be able to maintain or sustain in any way the work which God intends you to accomplish." Paul emphasizes this: "Mine own son after the common faith. . . . For this cause I left thee in Crete, that thou shouldest set in order the things that are wanting" (Titus 1:4–5).

There's a fascinating emphasis that's placed here. God setting in order the church of apostles, prophets, and teachers. He sends Titus as a bishop, teacher, *episcopos* or ruler, over the flock of God. He instructs him to ordain authority in the church. Who was doing the ordaining? Titus. By whose authority? Paul's. What was the purpose? To make sure that the authority of the church is maintained about the Word of God.

Don't get away from it. Do it this way.

Sometimes, we don't like to hear that. We like to have a congregational vote where 52% of the people raise their hands and we dutifully say, "That's what God wants." Biblical theology doesn't teach this kind of nonsense. One percent of the people may have what God wants, and 99% of the rest are kooky!

In fact, my dealings with churches over a long period of time indicate that every time I get a majority, I instantaneously become suspicious. I want to examine the motivation because percentage does not determine God's will.

Q: *Feelings seem to have trumped authority in the church today. Why is this such a problem?*

Without authority in the church, you are not going to have power. The Spirit of God will not act independent of the Word. If you don't know the Word, you are not going to get the power.

Do you expect God to violate everything He said so you can have a nice warm feeling? Well, forget it, because that's not the way He does it. We've gotten away from authority in the church. That's why we have the shepherding movement. That's why we have divisive charismatics all over the place. That's why we have a crisis in charismatic theology today, because there is not a polarization around the authority of Holy Scripture. Someone gets up in a pulpit and has a nice warm feeling about something, and we tend to say, "Oh praise the Lord." I tend to say, "Yuck!"

If your nice warm feeling does not correlate with Holy Scripture, stow it—get rid of it. It's not what God is saying.

We don't like to hear these things; they disturb us. Good! Get disturbed, because without authority in the church, you are not going to have power.

Q: *Didn't Peter leave his wife and his children to follow Jesus?*

No, he did not. The Apostle Paul says that Peter brought his wife with him. Paul asks, "Do we not have the right to take along a believing wife, as do the other apostles and the brothers of the Lord, and Cephas?" (1 Cor. 9:5, ESV). This indicates that several of the apostles were married during their ministries. So, if he took his wife with him when he preached, obviously he didn't abandon his wife. Christ didn't tell His disciples to abandon their families.

Interestingly enough, we also have an account from Eusebius of the death of Peter's wife—on the same day Peter was crucified upside down:

> They say, accordingly, that when the blessed Peter saw his own wife led out to die, he rejoiced because of her summons and her return home, and called to her very encouragingly and comfortingly, addressing her by name, and saying, "Oh thou, remember the Lord." Such was the marriage of the blessed, and their perfect disposition toward those dearest to them.[1]

Q: *Please explain what Paul meant in Romans 13:8 when he said, "Owe no man anything." Should Christians and churches use credit or go into debt?*

It's good to read the context of the passage. It starts with "Don't owe anybody anything" but you must read the next part of it, "love one another for love is the fulfilling of the law." It's talking about living a relationship under the law as the Jew did, where he was always in debt to somebody either financially or as a result of their dealings or actions, their way of life, or their culture. What is really being said is don't put yourself under obligation to anyone so that they are able to get you to do what they want you to do rather than what you ought to do.

When we are under obligation to people, we do things for them that we would never do ourselves, simply because of the

1 Phillip Schaff and Henry Wace, eds., *A Select Library of Nicene and Post-Nicene Fathers of the Christian Church* (New York: The Christian Literature Company, 1890), 162 (quoting Eusebius).

obligation. All you're being told here is, don't owe anyone to the point where they control you.

It doesn't have to do with banks or lenders, that would come under the law. Usury is a crime in the Bible. Christians are not to take exorbitant interest from other Christians, any more than Jews could charge interest on loans to their fellow Jews—it's forbidden.

I'll never forget, I was sitting at lunch with this very affluent Christian businessman, and he was telling me how difficult it was to diversify his assets. I long for the day I will have that difficulty myself! He was in the area that day diversifying his resources, and he said, "Well, I'm going to pick up a note owed me next week. I'm getting 22 percent interest."

I said, "That's interesting. Tell me, is the man a brother?"

"Oh yes, it's a Christian ministry."

I told him, "You can't do it."

He said, "What do you mean I can't do it?"

"You cannot take usury of a brother."

"That's not usury."

I said, "Oh yes, it is usury."

So, we had a knock-down usury fight.

He's a godly man. We finished dessert, leaned back, and he said, "Well, that's 22 percent I won't get," and he didn't take it.

Parents who loan their children money and charge them interest is another source of irritation to me. You may ask, are there people like that? Yeah, there are clods like that around trying to teach their children responsibility. You're not teaching them responsibility; you're teaching them—at an early age—to squeeze everyone because you're squeezing them.

Q: *How do you avoid false teachers? How do you tell sheep from wolves? How do you tell fleece from fur?*

If you run your life by comparing your experiences in spiritual matters to other people's experiences in spiritual matters, and if you spend your life weighing experience against experience, you are never going to learn anything. You're supposed to get into the Word of God, the sound foundation, the immovable rock. And once there, with your spiritual feet grounded in Holy Scripture, you test everyone that comes down the pike—no matter who they are.

You don't condemn them; you love them for Christ's sake, but you test them because it's your soul and your mind into which the poison will go, and if you can't tell the difference, you're in trouble—big trouble. If you don't know the Word of God well enough to know the difference between the wolves of destruction and the sheep of God's sheepfold, you are going to be one confused person. If you can't tell fleece from fur, look out! You are a prime candidate for doctrinal corruption.

All the teachers in the church are to be tested by each other in the light of the Word of God. They are to be tested by the history of the church and her pronouncements on the great doctrines of the Bible. There's no such thing as instant teaching authority. We are told never to lay hands on a man suddenly (1 Tim. 5:22), nor to exalt a novice (3:6). Do you know why? Because if they're mixed up in their thinking, they may eventually mix up your thinking! I don't care how sweet they are, or how many miracles are attributed to their meetings. I don't care about all the folderol of publicity kits, television appearances and other things that are used to promote people in the world of religious huckstering.

I'm only concerned with one thing: is it scriptural? Will it stand up? If it won't, jettison it. If it will, defend it. But at least have brains enough, determination enough, confidence enough in yourself, the Word of God and the Holy Spirit not to let somebody sell you something just because it sounds good.

Now, no doubt my words will be interpreted as hostility. That's right! I am eternally hostile to false teachings and you'd better be, too. Otherwise, they will disrupt your life and the lives of others.

Q: *What is the difference between the promises God made to physical Israel and the promises he made to the church in the New Testament?*

When the apostle Paul says that we are all the children of Abraham by faith, he is using Abraham as an example of faith. We are his children by faith. We are not the actual physical children of Abraham, but Christians are the spiritual children of Abraham and heirs according to the promises that God made to him. Now, that doesn't mean that the church inherits the promises of national Israel because it is a very clear distinction biblically between national Israel—the establishment of the Davidic throne on the earth—and the Church of Jesus Christ. It's a very clear differentiation. You're not going to make the church national Israel.

Q: *If Jesus said not to swear an oath, why do we see oaths taken later on in the Bible? Romans 1:9 tells us, "For God is my witness..."; also Second Corinthians 1:23; 11:31; Galatians 1:20. How do these oaths stand in relation to Matthew 5:33, 37 and in James 5:12?*

They're not oaths. Paul is not saying I am swearing by God Almighty. He says, "I am telling you God will bear witness for me when the time comes." That's not an oath; that's simply pointing out that God will bear witness or tell the truth. I often say in the middle of a discussion, "As the Lord lives . . ." and that's not an oath; that's simply an affirmation that this is true just as God is true in life. So, we're not talking about oaths in those contexts.

What Jesus was talking about was swearing by the temple, swearing by God, swearing by the throne, swearing by the hairs of your head, swearing by anything. Jesus said don't swear at all; don't perform an oath. That is something where God says we should let our yes be yes and our no be no.

Q: *Do you think someone can have the gift of healing today, just like the apostles and Jesus?*

Yes, I think there are people that exercise the gift of healing and the gift of miracles today. I don't think they exercise it the way Christ did because Christ was God in human flesh. Anyone that Jesus touched or prayed for was healed. The apostles prayed for some people, and they weren't healed.

I rather doubt the apostles healed everyone because Paul left Epaphroditus sick for three months at Troas, and he himself was ill with an eye affliction that never left him, according to church history.

Paul also makes reference to others who were ill, and some who died as a result of illnesses—even though he had prayed for them. So, I do not think that you can argue that the apostles healed as Jesus did. Christ healed everyone. They couldn't heal everyone and we can't, either.

Q: *What about the argument being used today that the gift of healing doesn't exist after a certain time in church history?*

I'm primarily concerned with the text of Scripture. The text of Scripture specifically states that during the time of Christ, He healed everyone He wanted to heal because He had the power to do so. We also learn from Scripture that the apostles prayed for people and there were miraculous healings, but not everyone was healed.

Church history reveals that the church sanctioned prayer for the sick, and that God honored that many times, and many people were healed. So, to argue that the gifts of healing are no longer in the church today is to fly in the face of church history and of contemporary experience. For instance, I can give a personal testimony. I laid hands on sick people in faith believing, and trusted

God for their healing, and they were miraculously healed—just as miraculously as anything ever done in the New Testament.

You can have the gift of healing if God wants to give it. If you say that God cannot do something today that He did two thousand years ago, you are limiting omnipotence.

Q: *Is the gift of healing, as exhibited by Pat Robertson on the 700 Club, spiritual?*

He believes in divine healing, and he prays for the sick, and I think that's biblical. He also anoints people, and I believe that's biblical. I'm not so sure that you can call out people's specific illnesses in auditoriums because I've seen that backfire. Therefore, I'm a little suspicious of the people that find themselves doing this on a regular basis.

I've heard him say, "There's someone listening to this broadcast who has a back problem," so you could say he's on perfectly safe ground—half the people in the country have back problems!

Q: *On August 20th we gave birth to our son, Mario. He is our first child and the first grandson on both sides of the family. Our pediatrician told us our son has a 90 percent chance of having Down Syndrome. We will know the test results in one week. We would like to ask that your class would lift him up in prayer and the test results will show that he is normal. We praise God for this blessing of having a child but deep inside it tears us up when we think about what he might have. We both trust in the Lord's purpose, and we just lift him up in prayer.*

The Lord can heal that child in the womb of the mother if it's a Down Syndrome baby. If the child is born with Down Syndrome, then we're to love and care for that child. We are to teach the child to understand the gospel and believe in Jesus Christ.

It is better to be a Down Syndrome child believing in Jesus Christ than to be a PhD from Berkeley who is an agnostic—much better. I wouldn't argue that point or debate it at all. Yes, we will pray for that child right now. Let's bow before the Lord in prayer:

> *We worship thee, our Father, the only living and true God, in Jesus Christ, whom thou hast sent, and we ask now and lift up before Thee on the altar of prayer this child, Mario. Encourage and strengthen these dear people that they may reach forth in faith believing that it is you who are working all things together for good to them that love you, to them who are called according to your purpose. If we ask anything in accordance with your will, you hear us. Hear us now and heal, O Lord, if this is necessary. In Jesus' name, Amen.*

Q: *What is positive confession? Why don't you believe in it?*

It's the idea that the power of life and death is in the tongue. Whatever you confess with your tongue, you will get. So if you confess good things, you get good things. If you confess bad things, you get bad things.

This doctrine was originated by Mary Baker Glover Patterson Eddy in a book entitled *Science and Health, with Key to the Scriptures*, published in 1875. This book is the core of Christian Science, Unity, Religious Science, Christ Unity Science, and all of the metaphysical Gnostic cults.

The Bible does not teach that you may confess health, wealth, prosperity, or evil to yourself. That is out of context and the Christian Scientists popularized it. Unfortunately, it has been picked up today by Christians.

Q: *What is your opinion of Dave Hunt's book,* Peace, Prosperity and the Coming Holocaust?

Some of it is good and some of it isn't. You should read it all in the light of Scripture and test it by the Word of God.

Q: *Is the church a public place?*

Yes, it is. This building is not the Church of Jesus Christ. It may seem like a joke to some people visiting us, but it isn't. No church building is the Church of Jesus Christ. It is a public auditorium. We—God's people—are the Church of Jesus Christ and shortly the church will go home to dinner, and this will be a building again. End of discussion. Why should we get so upset about it? It's only a building consecrated to God. You are the church.

Q: *What is your opinion on limited atonement?*

I do not accept the idea of limited atonement. That is part of what is known as Calvin's Tulip: Total depravity, Unconditional election, Limited atonement, Irresistible grace, and the Perseverance of the saints. I don't believe in limited atonement because First John 2:2 says that Jesus Christ is the satisfaction for all our sins.

It's pretty obvious that this is an epistle written to the church, so "our" must refer to the church, and John goes on to say not ours only but the sins of the whole world. So, Christ died for the sins of all mankind. If men do not accept the atonement then obviously, it does not provide redemption for their sins.

That's my position on the subject. I know the Calvinists don't hold this position and there are modified Calvinists in this area, and the Arminians don't hold it at all. However, that's the position that I take.

Q: *Do we have our own personal guardian angels?*

Scripture says that the servants of the Lord constantly are attended by his angels. Psalm 103:21 says they are ministering spirits. The Bible says they are sent forth to guard, protect or to watch over those who are the heirs of salvation, so I believe angels are agents of the Holy Spirit in accomplishing certain things in our lives. There is no doubt about that in the Scriptures.

All you have to do is get Billy Graham's book *Angels* (Word Books, 1986), or Dr. A.C. Gaebelein's book, *What the Bible Says About Angels* (Baker, 1987), and you will see the function of angels. Yes, I believe the angels do guard and watch over the Lord's people, particularly children, because Jesus said, "See that you do not despise one of these little ones, for I say to you, that their angels in heaven continually behold the face of My Father who is in heaven" (Matthew 18:10, NASB). So, we praise and thank the Lord for this continuing ministry of angels.

I believe in the ministry of angels, but I think we've got to be careful about books such as *Angels Unawares*, where the angels teach theological error—then you know that you are not dealing with guardian angels. Remember there are two kinds of angels—the good ones and the bad ones—and you've got to know what the difference is between them and how to tell the difference between them.

Q: ***I received a computer letter in the mail from a ministry. It said, "Dear computerized name, today my wife and I were thinking of you." I was sure in the next two paragraphs someone was going to hit me up for money.***

They were thinking of you? Is it wrong to ask for money to support the Lord's work? No, but it's wrong to lie to get that money. That ministry leader and his wife were no more thinking of you when they wrote that letter than they were thinking of the price of beans in Brazil. They were thinking of the money their letter would bring into the organization. It is evil to say "I'm thinking of you" while collecting money and not really thinking of you at all. That's evil.

Q: *What do people mean by the term "Christian ethics"?*

There is such a thing as Christian ethics. How many of you know what an ethic is? Let me tell you. A Christian ethic is a method of performance. In other words, you are saying I believe that Jesus Christ is the Son of God, right? Right! Perform. Don't lie. Don't cheat. Don't steal. Don't con people. Don't promote false doctrines. Don't live a double standard. That's the ethical requirement of the Christian.

If you say, "I love Jesus," don't jack up your price when you're repairing somebody's house or car. If you love Him, then don't figure out a way to make more money on a business deal that's not legitimate, moral, or right. That is the ethical requirement. If you claim to teach on the faculty of a school, and you're ethical, you don't sign doctrinal statements you don't believe in to keep your job; that's Christian ethics.

What's missing today in the ministry, in education, in the pulpit, and in the pew is good, old, simple performance. Do it, don't talk about it.

I'm sick of people running loose on the landscape of television. I turn off more Christian programs than I can keep track of because all I get on there is the sticky, syrupy junk that passes as Christian love while overlooking every issue of life. They never face it. Doesn't that get to you? It gets to me! You've got to have a reaction if you're really awake.

If you can walk down Hollywood and Vine, in the heart of Hollywood, and look at the pornography and filth that's there, and just shake your head and say, "That's terrible"—and then just walk away—then something's wrong. It should bother you.

If they open an X-rated theater in your neighborhood, and you just say, "That's awful, I certainly don't agree with that," and that's all you ever do—what good are you? You've got to act!

I know a Christian who shut down one of these theaters in his town in northern California. He saw it getting ready to open and he got all the Christian pastors with guts together. He got all the Christians he could get from all of the churches. They had a mass rally and picketed City Hall with signs such as, "Keep filth out of our community!"

Do you know what happened? They won! They stopped it in its tracks. We as Christians can get things done if we really want to stand up there and let people shoot at us.

Now if you happen to be of such a mild and tender nature that anything you run into in the form of conflict is going to upset you, well, obviously stay home and pray, but don't get in the way of the people who want to do it. Encourage them.

Jerry Falwell and I don't agree in certain areas, but where Jerry Falwell stands on the subject of morality in the media and against the pornography, evil, and corruption that exists today in the United States, is where every Christian ought to be standing. Everyone—even if you don't agree with some of the things he says. Thank God for someone who's taking a stand. If you don't stand for something, you'll fall for anything.

Q: *Was Mary sinless as the Catholics teach?*

No. She said in Luke 1:47, "My spirit has rejoiced in God my Savior." Savior means Deliverer, Redeemer—one who frees you from sin. Mary confessed herself before the angel of the Lord that she was a sinner, but she found grace in the sight of God. She knew she was a sinner. She also died and the wages of sin is death, physical as well as spiritual.

Q: *Was Peter the first pope?*

If he was, he didn't know it! No, he was not the first pope. He couldn't have been the first Pope, because the apostle Paul argued with him on a matter of faith and morals, contradicted him, and told him he was wrong—and Peter owned up to it. A pope is supposed to speak infallibly in matters of faith and morals, but Paul overruled Peter. Therefore, Peter was not the pope of the early Christian church.

The person who would have qualified as "pope" or top leader of the early church was Paul—or, in Jerusalem, perhaps James—not Peter. So, I wouldn't get too upset about it. Read Peter's own account of this in First Peter 2:5, where he says everyone is a little rock built up into a spiritual temple. "You also, as living stones, are being built up as a spiritual house for a holy priesthood, to offer up spiritual sacrifices acceptable to God through Jesus Christ" (NASB). Christ is the foundation stone of the church, not Peter.

Q: *Doctrinally, what does the Assembly of God believe?*

The Assembly of God are spirit-filled Baptists. They have two areas of disagreement with me. First, they believe *everyone* must speak in tongues as the initial evidence of baptism in the Holy Spirit. On this we agree to disagree agreeably—I don't agree and they agree that I don't. I will give you excellent reasons why I think it's not true and good AG pastors will tell you why it is true. We could debate the thing forever and never reach an agreement. It has nothing to do with our salvation or our fellowship in the Lord. That being the case, we should let it go and get about the business of preaching the gospel and fellowship in the body of Christ.

The second point we don't agree on is salvation: The Assembly of God believes that you can lose your salvation and get it back again. I believe that once you are truly regenerate you always belong to Christ. If you continue in sin, the Lord will destroy your body in order to redeem your soul. So we have differences of opinion in these primary areas of peripheral theology, but basically in every major area the Assemblies of God is doctrinally right on. Otherwise, I wouldn't teach in the Assembly of God Church if I didn't believe that.

Q: *Do you feel that friction between conservative dispensationalists and liberal charismatics will cause a schism in God's church?*

I don't think you can ever have a successful schism in God's church because the Scripture says that the gates of hell will not prevail against it (Matt. 16:18). That means that the meanness and pettiness of men will not prevail against the church either.

There are dispensationalists who are vigorously anti-charismatic, and there are some charismatics who at times get vigorously anti-dispensational. That does not alter the fact that both are members of the body of Christ, and that the Spirit will work in both of them as they are willing to yield to Him.

I don't worry too much about splits of that nature. I rather say that the Lord will work out the details of it; all we have to do is be faithful where we are and let Him take care of all of the rest of the things. It's when we start getting in the picture and mucking it up that things get confused and schismatic in the church.

There are genuine schisms, or more serious divisions, in the church. Paul says there have to be at some point so that the truth might be known. There must be arguments and divisions among you, partings of different opinions, he says in Corinthians, so that the truth may come out. What a terrible church it would be if everyone dressed the same, talked the same, decorated their houses the same, or had the same vocabulary all the time. It would be nauseating within a short period of time.

Look at the infinite variety of people—just in your church—that God, in his mercy, has been pleased to create. We are living proof that He has a sense of humor! People sometimes say to me why do you mix humor with theology? Because it needs it. You have to be able to laugh, in the midst of this cosmic zoo where we live.

Q: *In your opinion, did Joseph Smith actually encounter the angel Moroni, or was Moroni a figment of his imagination?*

I think Smith probably had supernatural encounters, but they were not from the Holy Spirit because of the doctrine he got out of it. He could have been a man misled by demonic forces, or simply a con man who used religion to promote his own views—or a combination of both. It could have been satanic, and appealed to his carnal nature, so he went for it.

I think he knew on some level that he did not get divine revelations that would replace Christianity. He was terribly deluded.

Q: *In discussing the bodily resurrection of Jesus Christ with a Jehovah's Witness, she said that Jesus went through walls. I didn't know how to answer. What would you say?*

It doesn't say anywhere in the Bible that Jesus went through walls, floors, ceilings, doors, or anything else. The only passage you have is in John 20, when the disciples were in the upper room after the Resurrection. Jesus appeared in the room. It does not say He came through the walls, floors, ceiling, windows, or anything else. It simply says He appeared there.

Now, you've got to remember something: in His resurrection, Christ possessed an immortal body. It wasn't an immortal body of flesh and bone. He could move from earth to heaven, from dimension to dimension, at the twinkling of an eye. He didn't have to pass through anything. As God manifest in the flesh, He could simply be there anytime He wished.

Try asking a Jehovah's Witness this question: where does the Bible say Jesus ever went through walls, floors, or ceilings? They can't show it to you. They'll take you to John 20, and all you need to do then is point out that the passage says Jesus appeared there.

It doesn't say how He appeared, so stop trying to make it something that it isn't. There are also a couple of other good explanations, but that one should get the conversation on the right track.

Q: ***I've been talking to a Mormon friend of mine about the false teachings of their church. Just when I thought some seeds might take root, he handed me the book,* A Marvelous Work and a Wonder *by LeGrand Richards. He said it would explain all of my questions on Mormonism. He told me to pray about the book and see if it is right. How can I gracefully show him the errors of this book? I'm now studying your book,* The Maze of Mormonism. *Have you checked Richards out?***

Yes, we checked Richards out, and the book is not "a marvelous work and a wonder"—nor is it Mormonism. It's a classic blunder in theology; Richards was not a theologian. The book is loaded with typical Mormon doctrine, so if you have *The Maze of Mormonism*, just simply take the doctrines that are there, see what Richards says, and you will immediately find the documentation that proves it is definitely a non-Christian cult.

As far as answering Richards' arguments, he's been answered many times by many writers on the subject of Mormonism. I answered him, too. The book is weak, and I wouldn't get too upset about it. Just simply compare it with *The Maze of Mormonism* and then with the text of Scripture.

One thing more: this Mormon told you to pray about the book to see if it's true? Do you hear that? That's experience talking; that's emotion talking. It's not Scripture talking. You do not pray about something you know God has already said, you pray about what you don't know. If God has said it, you don't need to pray about it. If the Lord says, "Thou shalt not steal" and you get a great opportunity to steal, you don't say, "I'm going to pray about this and find out whether or not, just this once, I can get away with it." That's not biblical theology.

You don't pick up the *Book of Mormon* and say, "I'm going to pray about this to see if it's true." You put the *Book of Mormon* next to Holy Scripture, and you will know whether it's true or false. God has already spoken on the subject.

So, the next time a Mormon asks if you've prayed about the *Book of Mormon*, ask them if they've prayed about the Vedas or the Koran, and they will just look at you. Have you prayed about the Koran? If they say they haven't, just ask them, why not?

They will say they've found the truth—they have the witness in themselves—and that's when you ask, "How do you know you've found the truth?" The door is wide open then, and all you have to do is say, "Funny thing about that, I've got the witness in myself, too, and it says that Mormonism is a cult and the Bible condemns it. Isn't that amazing? Which witness is true—your experience or mine?"

They can't answer it, and that's when you say, "Let's go to the Bible and find out." Then, when you test it by the Bible, you know. Praise the Lord for the opportunity to witness to them, and keep on loving them.

Q: *What does the Church of Christ believe, and are they considered a cult?*

They're not considered a cult, but they have some very unbiblical teachings. The first is that you must be baptized by them in order to be saved. That is not biblical theology. They've already damned the Quakers, the Salvation Army, and anyone who won't be baptized by them. Anybody who won't be baptized at all is automatically lost according to the Church of Christ.

Secondly, they don't have instrumental music in their church because they say that's not New Testament theology. But in the Old Testament, the Jews worshipped God with timbrel, harp, lute—all kinds of music. Dancing and music were part of the worship service. There's no reason to suppose that this changed among the Jews in the New Testament. The church always had music from its earliest days.

The Church of Christ just grabbed onto something by saying we don't have church music. Wonderful for you. Isn't that great? What does that give you—some kind of status? Yes, they say, we're the only church that does that. That isn't status; that's an absence of intelligence. Talk to Pat Boone about this. He's a former member of the Church of Christ. He will tell you just how far out in orbit they are when it comes to this subject.

Q: ***Is it necessary for a Christian to be a member of a church? I alternate between two churches and your Bible study, usually attending both church and Bible study the same day.***

Well, I can't play Holy Spirit for people. You're to be in a local congregation where you're getting fed the Word of God and where you can function within the life of the church, have fellowship with those in the church, and become involved in church programs. I have found over the years that this is the best way to grow in grace and in spiritual maturity.

When I left Melodyland Christian Center and came here to Newport Mesa Christian Center, I told the class that one of the things I objected to the entire time I was there was that there was no basic church function in the entire place. It was a whole series of independent churches, and a great big pep rally on Sunday morning and afternoon, where you were never expected to think. You were only expected to get emotionally involved, and my objection for over seven years—I constantly made the objection—was that we should have participation on a church level that did not exist. That's why, when I came here and talked with Dr. Wood about it, I felt the Lord led me here, and I urged the people who came to affiliate with the church to have a good, solid relationship with the church.

I'm not a member of the Assemblies of God so I'm not pushing it as one of their ministers—I'm a Southern Baptist minister. I'm saying that since our Bible class is here at an AG Church, and if you have no other affiliation and you can agree with the position of the Assemblies of God, by all means be affiliated with the church. I believe it will be a greater spiritual blessing for you if you are. So, that's an altruistic recommendation, but it's something that's between you and the Lord. It's necessary for spiritual maturity to have a good church relationship.

Q: *Is it going against the Christian church for a woman to pastor a church?*

Pentecostals and Charismatics believe that women may exercise the office of pastor in the church. I do not believe this. I do not believe it for two specific reasons. First of all, the New Testament never, ever confers upon a woman the office of elder. Never. They may be deaconesses, but they may not be elders. That is very significant because the elders were pastors, so no woman was ever an elder in the early church or in the church's history until liberal theology began to take control in the last 40 or 50 years in American Christianity. The Pentecostals believe that women have this right because they saw gifts from the Holy Spirit manifested in women and they assumed that therefore it was right for the women to exercise spiritual gifts. And if that is the case, why not be evangelists and pastors?

Women may be evangelists. Philip's daughters were evangelists. To evangelize means to proclaim the gospel. Women may certainly do that and have a long record of doing a very excellent job of that in Sunday School, on the mission field, and in their neighborhoods and churches. I thank God for faithful women. But if we're getting to the technical point of the position of

Scripture on women as pastors, no evidence at all exists for it and all the evidence extant is against it. That's point number one.

Point number two is that the history of the church is against it from the first century on upwards. The church did not ordain women to the pastorate. The Roman Catholic Church and the Greek Orthodox church are both having a full-scale war today because they are standing in the tradition of church history in this area. They're right, and therefore they're getting a lot of flak from liberal theologians inside and outside of the church.

That's my position on it. I think the position can be sustained, and if you would like to discuss it with Dr. George Wood who takes the opposite position and is an equally qualified scholar, then you have the option to go chat with him. He and I chat from time to time in these areas, and we agree to disagree agreeably. Personally, I think it's a waste of time and energy to get into it.

Q:* *What does it mean to give 10 percent of your income regardless of your circumstances? I've been taught that principle.

In the Old Testament, the Bible says that you give God 10 percent. It was known as storehouse tithing. God said in Malachi 3:10, "'Bring the whole tithe into the storehouse, so that there may be food in My house, and test Me now in this,' says the Lord of hosts, 'if I will not open for you the windows of heaven, and pour out for you a blessing until it overflows'" (NASB). That was God dealing with Israel.

When we move into the New Testament, the church is never enjoined to tithe per se. The New Testament never mentions the word tithe connected with the Christian. However, you should follow a good, sound principle that God honored in the Old Testament. Remember that the church was in Abraham's loins when Abraham paid tithe to Melchizedek (Gen. 14:20) and we are Abraham's children. This is before the Mosaic law, so we could conceivably argue that since Christ is the high priest after the order of Melchizedek, we owe him the 10 percent even as Abraham owed 10 percent to Melchizedek.

But whether you believe it's enjoined upon you or whether you practice it voluntarily as a principle of the Old Testament or you accept the Melchizedek argument, the point is that you should begin giving to God by God's standard. That's the Old Testament. Give him 10 percent off the top.

If you think about it, you owe Him the other 90 percent, because He gave you the strength, capacity, and will to get everything you've got. So technically, everything under the whole canopy of space belongs to the Lord—everything. So why quibble with Him about 10 percent? Why not start with the 10 percent in the Old Testament and then work your way up as the Lord prospers you? You can't outgive God, and you'll get blessed out of your socks. The Scripture says, "Do not let your left hand know what your right hand is doing" (Matt. 6:3, NASB), so that means start with 10 percent, then give it away gloriously and let the Lord take care of it.

Q: *What if I don't have any money to give?*

The Scripture clearly states that the Lord intends us to fulfill the command to care for our own. Whoever does not care for those of his own household is worse than the infidel. He has denied the faith. So, you must take care of your family—your children—because that's a primary obligation given to you by God. It's not wrong to use your money for the needs of your children and your family's needs, and I don't believe Scripture forbids it.

There are those who disagree with me, and they say give the 10 percent anyhow, and God will provide. Well, there have been many instances where people have done precisely that, and it has not been forthcoming. Does that mean God didn't provide it?

No, it meant that God was trying to teach them something, and it was that caring for their family was their primary obligation. You must provide for those in your own household. The Lord is not going to take from you what is needed by your children. Never. Dr. Barnhouse used to say that if it's a choice between 10 percent to the Lord or a pair of shoes for your children, the Lord wants the children to have the shoes. Figure it into the 10 percent. That was his opinion, and he didn't believe in tithing at all. I have a modified view on the subject, but definitely not a legalistic view.

Q: ***Do you believe there should be any special dispensation made over leftover communion elements? I understand that in some Protestant churches they cannot be thrown away because they are sanctified.***

Well, remember that the elements for communion are simply bread and wine or bread and grape juice. They have no significance in and of themselves. The Catholic Church says that when you take the host at the consecration Mass, in that moment the body, soul, blood, and divinity of Jesus Christ is present in the act or appearance of bread and wine. So, down through the ages, we have gotten the idea that somehow or other the elements themselves have some special value. But the truth is they don't, any more than this building does.

For example, as soon as we leave here, the church will have gone home to eat dinner. This is not the church. This is a building sanctified for the service of God, but we are the church. Our presence sanctifies the building. At the Lord's table, when we take the bread and the wine, we are at that moment testifying to Christ's death until He comes; to His incarnation, to His death for our sins, to His resurrection from the dead, and to His second coming. He can't come back unless He's alive. So that is the significance of the Lord's table.

As soon as it's over, and we've had that communion with the Lord, the elements that are left are nothing more than the elements they were before. What sanctifies it is when we are taking it at that moment of commemoration to Christ.

When I attended Catholic school, I remember being told that when you take the host, be sure to cup your hands so that you don't hold it with your fingers, and then when you take it, stick your tongue out and lift the host from your fingers or from the cup of your hand onto your tongue. Do not chew it, but let it dissolve in your mouth and swallow it, because if you were chewing it, you were chewing the body and the blood of Christ. That's really carrying it far beyond anything that Scripture is talking about, but that goes to show you what you can end up believing if you want to press it. As far as the elements themselves are concerned, they are simply bread and wine or bread and grape juice, and should not occupy our thinking.

Q: ***At the Crystal Cathedral[2] they have unveiled a statue of Job suffering. Dallas Anderson, a Brigham Young University art professor who sculpted the Statue of Job, will join the cathedral staff full time in 1984 and begin work on the next two statues.***

Why should this surprise you? Norman Vincent Peale trucked his carcass to Salt Lake City and kissed the foot of Spencer Kimball. Norman Vincent Peale—the high priest of the power of positive thinking—went out there and paid homage to the president of the Mormon Church, calling him a great servant of God. This is the old devil who denies the Trinity, the deity of Christ, the blood of the cross, salvation by grace and justification by faith,

2 The Crystal Cathedral filed for bancrupty in 2010 and the ministry was dissolved by 2012. The property was sold to the local Roman Catholic Diocese of Orange.

and Peale is out there telling everybody the Mormons are great Christians. That's evil.

Good grief, what has happened to our sense of discernment? If the President of the United States, a very influential personality, were to throw his arms around the president of the Mormon Church and call him a dear brother in the Lord, with all the tremendous power of his office, would that change the fact that the man was evil? No, of course not. It wouldn't make any difference who endorsed him, he would still be evil.

We must understand that evil exists for the sake of evil, and it is opposed to God no matter who endorses it. Therefore, you don't want to be carried away by names, cathedrals, programs, prestige, pizzazz—all the stuff that passes for spirituality. What you want to do is ask yourself the question: is this person preaching Jesus Christ and will he or she defend the gospel? Are they teaching the truth?

Q: *Has the church learned anything from the evils of the past?*

Let me tell you something: I'm reliving the 1930s, back when I was just a mere boy. I'm reliving the mentality of the 1930s in the 1980s, almost 50 years after the fact. Do you know what the mentality was in America in the 1930s? "We've got to get out of this Depression; whatever is going to get us out of this Depression is good for us."

Great mistake. We're still paying for what was "good for us."

Today we are making the same mistake. Fifty years from now our great-grandchildren will be paying for it—deficit financing. History shows us it never works.

Adolf Hitler and Joseph Stalin were known to be mass murderers. They were known to be ruthless, evil men. This was an acknowledged fact in our country, and yet I can still hear the speeches on the radio. I can still see the articles in the paper telling everyone that we didn't have to worry about these people. "They're 3,000 miles away from us, and besides, Hitler has built autobahns. He's created the Volkswagen, and Germany's never been better off than it is now. Look at the miracles he's been able to accomplish."

And then there was Stalin. He took Russia from the age of the peasants and brought them into the five-year plan of mechanization. These are great accomplishments—done over the bodies of millions of innocent people. As a kid I sat there and shook my head and thought, *Something's wrong!*

Something's wrong today, fifty years later. Has the church learned anything from this at all? We are sitting here looking around at the grossest evils, and just shaking our heads and saying, "Something's wrong." Yes, something *is* wrong and we must do something about it. Move. That's what's important.

4

Daily Christian Living

Many people asked Dr. Martin questions about their personal walk with God. While seeeking to help them individually, he sought to frame his answers in a way that would provide guidance to other believers as well.

Q: *What does it mean to pursue God?*

I am a teacher. I have been set in the church for the purpose of teaching. You are to listen to what I say only insofar as what I teach is in accordance with Holy Scripture. You are not going to be able to do that unless you know the Word of God. The purpose of teaching is to get you to the place where you will know it. You are not going to be a miniature Walter Martin or anybody else. You are going to be you—filled with the Holy Spirit—immersed (pardon the reference to Baptist theology) in God's Word, and desirous of putting the Word into practical application through the spirit and in love, so people will see in our Crete today that Jesus Christ is alive.

That's the name of the game. Without it, there isn't any game worth playing. It is only a surface charade in which we mouth the words, quote the verses, and get the right expressions on our faces. We may think we're going to whoop up the Holy Spirit or haul Him down for a revival and God's going to do it because we feel that way. Bushwa! You are going to have a revival when the Holy Spirit breathes on you. He is not about to breathe unless you are pursuing Him in the Word of God.

Q: *I'm just one person. What can I do for God?*

I asked myself that same question twenty-seven years ago and the answer was, *Do what you can, to the best of your ability. Plant and water, and I will give the increase.* Twenty-seven years later the increase is all around me in my own country and the letters we receive from all over the world. You learn something from that. You should never say, what can I do? You should say, what can the Lord and I do together? You're not alone. All you have to do is take that step of faith.

Talk to that Jehovah's Witness, talk to that Mormon missionary, care about people enough to risk them getting mad at you, but tell them the truth. The people that will curse you and want to do violence to you when they're in the darkness of the cults, will later seek you out and hug you, kiss you, and bathe your breast with their tears because they have come out of darkness into God's marvelous light. That's worth it, isn't it? What are a few curses along the way?

Q: *Do you believe in the baptism of the Holy Spirit and in speaking other languages?*

I believe in the baptism of the Holy Spirit, and I believe it can be accompanied by tongues. I don't think you can prove biblically that it must always be accompanied by tongues.

First of all, the moment that you're born again you are baptized into the body of Christ by the Holy Spirit, you are filled with the Holy Spirit, and your body becomes the temple of the Holy Spirit. There's absolutely no doubt about this, according to First Corinthians 12. That's the first fact.

Secondly, there is described in the book of Acts what is known as baptism in the Holy Spirit, where the Holy Spirit comes upon the believer and manifests himself in spiritual gifts. This may occur at the moment of conversion, but most often it occurs subsequent to conversion and in the life of the believer as the believer draws near to Christ, then seeks Him.

Now, whether you call it enduement of power or baptism in the Spirit or the promise of the Father is irrelevant—you're dealing with synonyms. It is an act subsequent to redemption where God enables you to exercise spiritual gifts you did not have the power to exercise before.

Finally, the gifts and the calling of God, according to Romans 11:29, cannot be revoked, which means that they are here in the church until Jesus Christ comes back again. The only way you can get rid of the gifts of the Spirit is to revoke the call of God. If you can revoke the call of God, you can revoke the gifts.

Some people are trying to do it all the time and they ought to look at the context of Romans 11, where God is dealing with Israel. He's not revoked His call to Israel, and He's not going to revoke His gifts either! Let me also point out that the Reformers believed this—Luther, Calvin, and Wesley. All the great theologians of the church have believed this. Only since the rise of dispensationalism in the 1840s have people begun to question the perpetuity of spiritual gifts. It has always been a part of Eastern Orthodox, Catholic, and Reformation theology.

Q: ***Would you say that this baptism is something like giving your life more to God every day?***

I think it's something that occurs as you yield to the Lord and as you seek Him. First Corinthians 14:12 says, "Even so ye, forasmuch as ye are zealous of spiritual gifts, seek that ye may excel to the edifying of the church."

Q: ***I haven't been witnessing a lot. I'm a born again Christian and it's really hard when people ask me questions. Are there any passages that could help me with that?***

The Bible says in Second Timothy 2:15, "Study to shew thyself approved unto God, a workman that needeth not to be ashamed, rightly dividing the word of truth." You're just a baby Christian. Babies have to be fed and they have to grow. You need to be fed from the Word of God and from a good strong local Christian church. You need prayer, Scripture reading, and fellowship with more mature Christians. You need to grow in grace in the knowledge of the Lord Jesus. You need good literature and devotion to the Word of God.

It's a progressive thing. You're not going to have all the answers to everything immediately, and you shouldn't get discouraged.

Q: *Can our sins really be passed on to the third and fourth generation?*

Yes, if the third and fourth generations follow your sins. God says, "I will visit the iniquities of the fathers upon the children to the third and fourth generation," but they always stop quoting there; God goes on to say, "of them that hate me" (Exod. 20:5). That means the sins of the fathers go on to the children if the children proceed to hate God. Period. He doesn't punish the innocent for the crimes of the guilty (see Ezek. 18:20).

Q: *Does God have one person picked out for each individual to love and marry or are there several ones you could love and have a good marriage with?*

You know, I've never been able to figure out how He does it. The reason I can't figure out how He does it is because everybody falls in love so many times, and they keep telling us this is the one. Go back to when you were 16 years of age—she was the one. If you had gotten what you prayed for, would you be happy? No.

I do tend to believe that God has an ideal partner for us, and He exposes us to that person. The problem with us is we sometimes marry the wrong one. That happens. Christians can sin and make mistakes, and of course there's the second-best choice, and the third-best choice. I don't know how He runs it. I'm just glad that He's in it somewhere because if it's you and me, wow, what a mess we're going to have.

Q: *Isn't gambling just having fun?*

I was in Las Vegas recently and I used to be quite a gambler before I was a Christian. I asked myself how am I going to cope with Las Vegas and the things that are there? And yet, God called me to Las Vegas. So, I prayed, "Lord, when I get to Las Vegas, deliver me from my past sins." I got there, and I walked into a big casino in the hotel—slot machines everywhere including the bathrooms—and I didn't feel a thing because the Holy Spirit said to me, "Don't you dare put so much as one penny in those machines because it belongs to Me. I gave it to you, and I don't want to spend it in the slot machine!" That's a marvelous way to be instructed by the Holy Spirit.

Q: *I heard you were in Carson City, Nevada recently.*[1]

I have a wonderful praise report for you. I was in Carson City, Nevada, just a few miles from Sin City [Las Vegas]. I always stay away from there because I smell sulfur when I get within a hundred miles, and that always bothers me when I remember Sodom and Gomorrah. But at any rate, I was there; I was invited to go there by KNIS radio station. The manager of the station is a real turned-on Christian and he said, "I want you to come to Carson City and Reno—we cover the entire area. I believe if you come, we can fill up the biggest auditorium in Carson. We'll have a tremendous time!"

I arrived at this very large auditorium, and the place was absolutely mobbed with people. They'd driven in from as far as 100 miles away—it's a central area, Lake Tahoe, Carson City, and of course, Reno. It was literally wall-to-wall with people.

1 The questioner seems to imply that since Carson City is so close to Las Vegas, Walter Martin was awfully close to a gambling haven.

There were ex-cultists, ex-Mormons, ex-Jehovah's Witnesses, and—of all things—the son of L. Ron Hubbard, the founder of Scientology. This will really blow your mind. He was at this meeting! I got this beautiful handwritten letter after the meetings that said, in effect, "Dear Dr Martin, I've been attending your meetings on Monday, Tuesday, and Wednesday nights. I am the son of L. Ron Hubbard, the founder of Scientology. They were so good and you are right about everything—what you're saying is the truth. I've tried to expose L. Ron Hubbard and Scientology for years. I've been in the newspapers and media—there was even a big lawsuit to declare my father dead or mentally incompetent just last year. I want you to know I am a born-again Christian who loves the Lord Jesus Christ. I just sat back there in Carson City for three nights and watched the Holy Spirit roll. Praise God! I want you to know I am praying for you and praise God, He's going to carry us all through this."

Here is a fantastic thing—the son of the founder of one of the most dangerous of all non-Christian cults is born again and witnessing for Christ. I think that's a tremendously encouraging thing because it shows that the Lord is reaching people where you would never believe they could be reached.

I did a live *Bible Answer Man* radio program in the daytime for two hours on the station covering the area and the phone lines were jammed for twenty minutes before and thirty minutes after the program, which shows the interest of people. I'm just so happy to report that people are praising the Lord that someone is addressing the questions that are bugging them. The Christian church today is looking for answers.

Q: *How do we help friends and family who drink too much and don't know the Lord?*

My teacher, Dr. Barnhouse, never went near the stuff and couldn't stand it. Years ago, I would have been lapping it up, but no way, it just completely passed me by because God said, "That's mine. Leave it alone."

A man came up to Dr. Barnhouse one time at a wedding reception and said, "Would you like a highball?" And Dr. Barnhouse looked at him and said, "Just a moment. *Holy Spirit, would you like a slug of whiskey?*" The man almost fell on the ground in shock. Barnhouse finished, "No, He doesn't want any, and neither do I." Then he looked at the man whose mouth was open about a foot by now, whose glazed eyes had suddenly come to life, and said, "You know, when you don't have the Holy Spirit in your body, you've got to have other spirits, and that's your problem."

The man just stood there and Barnhouse sobered him up with Jesus Christ. Whether he got saved or not, I don't know, but that's not our concern. The results are God's business—doing the job is ours.

Plant the seed. Water it. Pray. Leave the decision and the fruit to God, and keep right on going.

Q: *I believe witnessing can change lives, so why does sharing my faith seem so discouraging at times?*

Did you ever watch sowers planting in a field? Take a good look at someone planting seed. Do they drop one seed, sit down, and wait for it to grow? Do they say, "As soon as it comes up, I'll go on to the next one?" No, you'd have to be some kind of a nut.

You throw the seed all over the place, mechanically or manually, because you're doing what? Planting. The rain eventually comes and nature takes its course. God ordained it that way. In the same way, he's also ordained the natural for us as Christians. The normal for us as Christians is preach the word. Stand up for the gospel. Water it. Pray and keep moving. If you have the opportunity, take care of the seed.

Too often we're discouraged because we don't see a great harvest out there. No farmer expects a harvest the next day. It has to come naturally. Just plant. That's all God wants us to do. Plant. Water. Stand up.

Q: *Why did the Pharisees and Sadducees get so mad at Jesus when he condemned them to hell for what they were doing?*

They taught that when you went to Sheol or Hades or Gehenna to get punished, that the term of punishment was 42 months—after which you were relieved and permitted to enter Abraham's bosom. That was Jewish theology, then.

Jesus came along and blew the whistle on the whole thing. He ruined it. He said I'm going to tell you what it's really like. If you turn from Me, the Messiah, you will endure your own Gehenna—everlasting fire. That is, you're going to get it forever. They did not take that too well. He ruined their theology on that particular point.

Q: *Is it wrong to tell your children that there's an Easter Bunny since it would be lying?*

No, it isn't lying—there are Easter bunnies in the stores! We were at church one Easter Sunday a few years ago and my little daughter, Debbie, wanted to see the live bunny they brought to the children's church.

"Isn't that a lovely Easter Bunny?" I said.

"That's not the Easter Bunny, Daddy. I met him last week."

Now, she was a very young child, so I was immediately interested in who she met last week.

I asked, "When did this happen?"

She said, "He came to school and I shook his paw."

What are you going to say? There is no Easter Bunny, but you shook his paw? You're dead, you just don't know what to say.

The Easter Bunny idea that's associated with Easter is relatively new. The symbol of the egg is rooted in ancient imagery of life and resurrection. It was used by the pagan religions and then taken over by Christianity. I would argue this imagery of Easter is a Romans 14 issue but I think we should leave room in life for imagination and fun.

Q: *Should we avoid using the word Easter to describe the Lord's Resurrection Day?*

Easter comes from the pagan word Estes, taken from a pagan goddess and the festival of spring. When the Christian church was exploding all over the world with the gospel and preaching, and people were being saved, they ran into all these pagan customs and cultures. So, the church decided not to fight the pagan custom and culture. Instead, they chose to simply confront it with Christ. Since the festival of spring was associated with Passover, the time that Christ died on the cross for our sins, Passover and the resurrection became almost synonymous in Christian theology and the Easter festival took over as a celebration. It was not a celebration of Estes and the Easter egg or any bunnies or even of the festival of spring—it was the celebration of the resurrection of Jesus Christ from the dead, and that automatically eclipsed all paganism on Sunday and on the day of the spring festival.

That's why you don't have that anymore, you have a celebration of the resurrection. There are lots of pagan origins but they have been obliterated. Some people may say, "Why keep a day like that—why keep Christmas?" That was another pagan date in the Roman Calendar. But if we follow that argument through to its logical conclusion, then why do we use Monday, Tuesday Wednesday, Thursday, Friday, and Saturday? Why say June, July, August, and so forth? All of these are drawn from the names of pagan gods and pagan cultures.

If you believe we shouldn't use Easter and Christmas, then go into work and stop writing Monday and Tuesday. Logically, you must be consistent when you reject pagan origins or give up arguing about it because we're stuck with historical pagan history, whether we like it or not. The nice thing about it is that Jesus Christ's resurrection wiped the whole mess out, and that's what counts.

Q: *Is there one book in the Bible that emphasizes practical Christian living?*

It is very clear that Titus is an exhortation to practical Christian living. The whole epistle is Paul telling a young man—ordained to be the ruling elder of a church in a horrible cultural context—how he is to live, what he is to do, and what the qualifications are for those who would be leaders and witnesses for the Lord Jesus Christ.

Have you ever wanted a practical manual on how to live it, what to do and what not to do? You get it in this shortest possible space. It is a brief excursion into the Christian life on the level of this is the way it is, do it—and that's exactly what Paul tells Titus.

Q: *I've got one of those confusing questions about divorce. I'm on my third marriage right now. I became a Christian halfway through my second marriage and things didn't work out, so we divorced. I'm kind of at a sticking point, as far as communion goes. I've asked the Lord's forgiveness for everything. I backslid pretty bad through the divorce and I finally came to the point where I realized that I had a choice. I could either sit back, be guilty, and stay away from the Lord or I could come back to being with him.*

The Scripture says in First John 1:9, "If we confess our sins, he is faithful and just to forgive us our sins and to cleanse us from all unrighteousness." If you are a Christian, God has wiped out all of the sins you committed in your marriage and He restores you through the power of the Lord Jesus Christ. Providing, of course, that you have done these things in a biblical manner.

"If we walk in the light, as he is in the light, we have fellowship one with another, and the blood of Jesus Christ cleanseth us from all sin" (1 John 1:7). But listen, don't shirk the Lord's table as long as you've confessed your sins. You can commune with the Lord, and He'll forgive you your sins.

Q: ***I know Masonry is a non-Christian cult but I'm in Job's Daughters—that's part of Masonry—and I'm a Christian. Job 42:15 says "In all the land there were no other girls that were like the daughters of Job." If we're good people and we mean to do good things, is it still okay to be part of it?***

The Bible is referring to the beauty of Job's daughters, so that's not really a biblical reason for being part of this group. If it is connected in any way with Masonry, I don't think I would be connected with it. Masonry is very definitely anti-Christian in a number of its tenets and practices. If you're associated with something like that, then I'd start looking at what they believe and what they're going to teach you. You better examine that material in the light of the Scriptures.

Q: ***How would you deal with a Christian brother who believes, and says he can support from the Scriptures, that social drinking with the boys is OK?***

There is no argument that will support drunkenness. There's an excellent argument that will support abstinence at least so far as testimony to the world is concerned. Romans 14 says we're not supposed to eat or drink anything that's going to cause a weaker brother to stumble or that's going to cause offense in the world, so that people will not come to Christ.

I know this is a very thorny area. We could probably spend a lot of time on it and generate more heat than light, but if you know that smoking offends other Christians, you should not smoke in their presence. In fact, you shouldn't smoke at all because you're defiling the temple of God.

The same is true with drinking to excess. Scripture forbids this to Christians in or outside of leadership. We're supposed to abstain from whatever it is that causes someone to trip in their Christian experience. This is the reason Paul says, "For if because of food your brother is hurt, you are no longer walking according to love. Do not destroy with your food him for whom Christ died" (Rom. 14:15, NASB). That's a very good maxim and he carried it out, and I think it's good for us, too.

Q: ***Who is the weaker brother? What is the reason, and can Christians enjoy wine in the privacy of their home without being a bad testimony?***

All kinds of little goodies could be discussed here, but I would just point again to Romans 14:22: "Happy is he who does not condemn himself in what he approves." Paul also said he would do nothing that would offend his brother. Those are very safe guidelines.

Of course, if you go to Italy, Italian Christians will set wine on the table for you, and if you don't drink the wine in the home of an Italian Christian, it is considered to be an insult. In fact, in any Italian home, if you don't drink the wine when it's presented to you, it's an insult.

I'll never forget the father of a good friend of mine, an unbeliever, who just delighted in chewing Christians up when they came to his house for dinner. He always presented them with a glass of wine, raised his glass and said, "*Salute*!"—which means "To your health!"—and of course, most of the Christians put down the glass and did not drink.

One night I came over to his home and the son introduced me. His father and I hit it off right away and when dinner came, grace was said, and he poured a glass of wine for himself and one for me. Silence came over the table as he passed it over to me.

I picked it up and said, "*Salute*!"

He said, "Ahhhh you're different from the rest of them. I can talk to you," and he swallowed the wine.

I said, "Good!" and I preached Jesus Christ to him for two solid hours. He never said a word. It cost me two ounces of red wine—that was a great bargain!

Someone might say, "I wouldn't do that." Well, "happy is the man who doesn't condemn himself." That was the only way I could get his ear and I got it, and he got a good witness. We became friends. Every time I came to the house I'd speak to him, and every time he'd see me, he'd say, "*Nessun inferno*!" ("No hell!") He associated my witness with hell! It's fascinating the way some people respond.

Q: *How can I be sure I'm "walking in the Spirit"?*

To walk in the Spirit means to be in conformity to the leading and the will of the Holy Spirit. How can you ascertain this? If you are filled with the love of God; if you have the joy of God's salvation and the peace that passes all understanding; if you have patience in the midst of tribulation and trials; if you have gentleness and the manifestation of goodness; if you are self-controlled; and if you are exercising faith, then you are walking in the spirit because He will not manifest these fruits unless you are walking with Him.

If these things are evident in your Christian experience, you know you are walking with Christ. You know that you have fellowship with each other and that His blood is right now continuing to cleanse you from all sin.

Q: *Does God punish us, as believers, if we refuse to walk with Him?*

The carnal mind is at war with God. The world that follows the flesh is God's enemy, and you can't be its friend. It is not subject to the law of God—it can never be. So if you are going to let your carnal nature rule your life, you will not be subject to God. You will be subject to punishment.

In Romans 8:8 we are told, "They that live in the flesh cannot please God." That's terrifying. It means the people whose life is a constant pursuit of the flesh can never please God. Anyone who does not have the spirit of Christ is not Christ's property.

Christians are not carnal, fleshly people—you walk in the Spirit if the Spirit of God dwells in you. The person whose life is dominated by the pursuit of the Spirit is governed by the law of the spirit of life in Christ Jesus, which is the love of God. They become more than conquerors through Him that loved us. I love Romans 8:9 (NASB)—"You are not in the flesh but in the Spirit, if indeed the Spirit of God dwells in you."

Q: *How do you store treasure in heaven?*

You do it by prayer, supplication, and thanksgiving. You store treasure in heaven by service to God, by presenting your body as a living sacrifice, holy and acceptable to God. You lay up treasure in heaven when you permit the fruits of the Spirit to blossom in your life: "love, joy, peace, patience, kindness, goodness, faithfulness, gentleness, and self-control" (Gal. 5:22–23).

You're allowing treasure to be stored for you when you allow the Holy Spirit to live in you and work through you to touch the lives of others. So, you want to know how to store treasures in heaven? Obey God now. Let the fruits of the Spirit, the power of the Spirit, and the life of Christ be part of your life.

Even a cup of water in the Master's name will not go without its reward. Let the life of Christ be lived in you.

Q: *What should I do if I'm angry with God?*

I'd take a good long look at my life and find out if I was playing with matches. That's the first thing I'd do. If that wasn't the case, the second thing I would do is go to the Lord and say, "I know, Lord, that it is you who, 'works all things together for good to them that love you and are called according to your purposes' (Rom. 8:28). I love you and I am called according to your purposes. Therefore, whatever is taking place in my life right now you will not allow to become so great that I can't handle it." God is faithful. He will not allow you to be tested beyond your power to resist (1 Cor. 10:13).

As far as being mad at God is concerned, it's totally fruitless. If you're offending God by your anger, you're being petulant. Jonah got mad at God—look at the end of the book—and God rebuked him.

If you're angry with God, the best way to deal with that is to get down on your knees and confess the sin. Tell Him you're sorry for being mad at Him, even though you're mad at Him still. Ask Him to help you not to be angry, and to forgive and restore you, and He will. He's so gracious, kind, patient, and loving to a race of people who are determined to pursue their own goals.

Q: *Sometimes, when I share my faith, it's frustrating. Nothing happens, no matter how many times I talk to the person.*

If men will not listen to Christ, if they will not listen to the Spirit, they're never going to listen to you or me. You can be the greatest preacher in the world, the greatest teacher, and the most dazzling logician. You can shatter people's arguments. You can give them unanswerable biblical rhetoric. You can quote verses from now until Purgatory freezes over. You can stun them with the knowledge of the Word of God—and that's all you'll do. You'll stun them, but they will not have received the message.

You and I are not in the business of impressing people with ourselves, with how much we know or our Christian testimony. We're in the business of communicating the meaning of that testimony to the lives of others. The only way we can do that is through the Holy Spirit. Every witness we have as believers is an encounter with Christ. As Luther so eloquently put it, you and I are His hands, His feet, His voice, His body, speaking to a dying world.

Q: ***Does it really make a difference if you worship on Saturday or Sunday?***

No, it doesn't. Colossians 2:16 is clear: "Let no man therefore judge you in meat, or in drink, or in respect of an holyday, or of the new moon, or of the sabbath days."

Q: ***How do you provide for your family and your children's future in this spiraling inflation in keeping with "Lay not up for yourselves treasures upon earth, where moth and rust doth corrupt" (Matt. 6:19)?***

When Christ said not to store up for ourselves treasures on earth, He was not talking about a person providing for his family. God already said in Second Thessalonians 3:10 that we have a moral and spiritual responsibility to provide for our families. He said that whoever does not provide for those of his own household is worse than the infidel. He has denied the faith because the faith obviously insists that you provide for your loved ones. He that does not provide for those of his own household is worse than the infidel—he's denied the faith.

At any rate, the point is that God insists that you provide for those of your household. So obviously, you would save for your children's education or save to pay your bills and provide for your family. Christ isn't talking about that. He's talking about your life being motivated by storing up riches. If that's all that motivates you and all that life means to you, Jesus has a word for you. He says that wherever your treasure is, there will your heart be also (Matt. 6:21). So, if your treasure is earthly, your heart is earthbound.

Q: *What if you have a responsibility to the company you work for? You're out there working and providing, and you have a better future if you stay with that company, but it's a lot of long hours. How do you scripturally say to yourself that it's okay to be putting in all those hours?*

If a man is putting in extra time to advance himself in the company for a short period of time, I can't see anything wrong with that. If he's trying to attain a specific goal like saving for a college education for his children, I don't see why that would be a problem. If, however, he's a workaholic and he neglects his family just to make money in the company, then that is contrary to Scripture.

Q: *I know God has forgiven my sins because of Jesus, but sometimes I feel so condemned when I remember the things I've done.*

If you go through the commands of God, you will see how all of them are consummated in love. Love is not some sticky, gooey emotional substance cooked up by theologians as an excuse for doing almost anything. God expressed love in Jesus Christ. This is the ultimate expression of love: "Love one another as I have loved you" (John 13:34).

We should not condemn ourselves for past sins—we are clean in the sight of God when we've asked for forgiveness and changed how we live our lives. The law of God cannot touch the Christian because the Christian has already died in Jesus Christ and risen again. We are not under the law, we are under grace—God's rule of the spirit of life through Christ Jesus (Rom. 8:1).

I wonder if we recognize exactly what's happened? God is saying to us: I will not hold you before my throne for eternal judgment. I will not charge your sins to your account. I have already charged them to Jesus of Nazareth, and I have given you my spirit so that you may walk with me in the light, having fellowship with each other—in the blood of Jesus Christ—that goes right on cleansing us every day from sin (1 John 1:7).

If we love each other as Jesus loved us, we will have no difficulty fulfilling the righteousness of the law. We will be fulfilling everything that God demands if we are loving Him and our neighbor as ourselves. The law of the spirit of life in Christ Jesus is the law of love, and it has set us free from sin and death.

Q: *With the rise of inflation and everything else, there seems to be a trend towards people living together to cut the cost. Is there anything in Scripture that could help us make a decision as to whether or not a male and female could room together if they are not boyfriend and girlfriend?*

Well, Scripture says in First Thessalonians that we are to avoid all forms of evil (5:22). It's translated in the King James as appearance, but the word is actually forms. What the Christian has to do is to judge his or her behavior on how it may affect the lives of others who are watching, Christians, and non-Christians. If a man and a woman are living together in today's culture, they may open themselves up to the suspicion of immorality.

Now, I can see circumstances where it could be permitted. They would be very limited circumstances, but it could happen. Let's say if a student had a home and rented out rooms in that home to people of both sexes. Students do this all the time and no one thinks anything of it. Some students move into houses, and they share a bathroom facility and the kitchen. Others have separate rooms of their own with a separate bathroom facility. So, it depends upon the circumstance itself.

Q: *I know we're not supposed to build up treasures on earth but in these times of inflation, is it all right for a Christian to invest in diamonds or real estate?*

There's nothing wrong with Christians making business investments in gold, diamonds, houses or whatever it may be, as hedges against inflation, if they have the resources to do so. If they are husbanding their resources as a means of future help for their family or independence for themselves when they reach retirement, I would think that any form of investment would be justifiable providing it was consistent with Christian ethics and morality.

I don't think God is against that. I think what God is speaking about is don't lay up treasures for yourself on earth. Don't let your heart, soul, mind, and your very being be so involved with what you're doing here on earth that you forget that, ultimately, the things that count are the things you do for God here on earth.

Christ said that where your treasure is, there will your heart be also. So, if your treasure is in houses or land or in diamonds and gold—all the things of earth—that these things are actually an end in themselves rather than a means to a greater end, both for your family and for yourself. They do not support the advancement of the kingdom of God by helping support the work of God. If that happens to you, so that they become the end goal, then it is a sin. If your treasure is there, your heart is going to be there also, and God says you're going to be barren of spiritual resources. Lay up for yourselves treasure in heaven.

Q: *Should we pray for homosexuals?*

Some people make fun of homosexuals and don't realize the problem. They don't realize the sin. They don't realize what the person is locked into. It's lethal, and God is going to deal with them, and we don't want God to deal with it as He did with Sodom and Gomorrah. We want Him to deal with it in compassion and love. That's got to be through the church—Christ's body. We've got to do it. We ought to pray for people like this.

Q: *I have a friend who constantly repeats church gossip. Any suggestions for dealing with this?*

If anyone raises questions about someone else or repeats rumors in your presence, then be a good Christian and stop scandal by not allowing it to circulate. That's the way you stop it. If someone says, "Did you hear about so and so?" You say, "No and furthermore, I don't want to."

Remember, "There are six things that the Lord hates; seven that are an abomination to him"—in this particular case, it's the talebearer and he that sows division among brothers (Prov. 6:16–19).

Q: *Can you give an example of spiritual warfare?*

A constant in some Christian lives is that people live yielded to sin—enslaved by something they cannot escape apart from the grace of God. When Christians are trapped in this sin, Scripture warns, "Let not sin therefore reign in your mortal body, to make you obey its passions" (Rom. 6:12).

You can read Scripture a hundred times and it still says, "Thou shalt not steal."

But if you proceed to go right on stealing and keep right on reading the Scripture, it is apparent that you are yielded to sin and not to God, no matter how much you read the Scripture.

Unfortunately, in some churches today, there is a corrosive disease that eats away at the holiness that God wants to give to the church. It is the disease of saying, "I do commit such and such a sin. It bothers me, but nobody's perfect. I confess it to the Lord, and I'm just trusting him to take it away."

Do you know what that breeds? More sin, more yielding to Satan and to the flesh. It does not yield victory to the Christian. If you confess the sin and you don't forsake the sin, you are still practicing the sin.

It amazes me how we sometimes think that we are eternal beings no matter what we do, and that God somehow has the phone off the hook in heaven, and what's going on isn't really seen on the big TV monitor.

Who do you think you're fooling? He who knows if the sparrow falls and if you drop a hair on your shoulder. He's not going to forget what you did last Saturday night, and you will live to be reminded of it.

Are you practicing sin? Confess it, and after you have confessed it, give it up, and God will give you the grace to escape it every single time. He will not permit you to be tested beyond your power of resistance.

Yield yourselves unto God. Give way to God and let the Lord handle your problem.

Q: *Is spiritual warfare personal warfare?*

The Bible clearly tells us there is such a thing as spiritual war. It's our warfare: it's personal war. It's not against people, it's against the rulers of the darkness of this age, who manipulate people as if this were a great chessboard on earth, and the forces are arrayed against the Christian church.

Now, of course, you have an option: you can be dumb. You can say, "I don't have any spiritual war, I think positively all the time. I don't have negative thoughts. I think only about possibilities and the things God has for me. There's no war around me." That's reminiscent of the Christian Scientist in hell who sat by himself in a corner and said, "I'm not here, I'm not here, I'm not here." But it never changes the fact—you're there! You are in a spiritual war whether you think so or not. The whole world is blowing up around you and you just can't sit there and say, "Nothing's happening."

It is—and it will continue to happen because the moment you enlist in the army of God you personally become a target. No more Mr. Nice Guy. You are on the satanic hit list. You are in the army of God.

If you will not fight in the army of God, then the Lord will discipline you until you get to the place where you will fight. You will get so many attacks that you will eventually have to do something. That is a warning. It is also biblical theology.

You are in the middle of a war. People who walk around in the middle of a war acting as if there is no war are called casualties. There are people scattered all over the landscape who are ineffective in their Christian lives, neutralized in their Christian witness, paralyzed in their Christian activities simply because they don't realize they're casualties. They must be restored by God so they can get back into the battle.

Q: *I have a friend, and she says she's born again, but she keeps using God's name in vain and she keeps sinning. I was wondering if anything will happen to her, and if you think she'll go to heaven?*

First of all, if someone told me they were born again, and all they did was swear and use bad language, I wouldn't believe them because whoever is born of God doesn't practice sin as a habit in their lives. It isn't something that dominates them. They can fall into sin but it's not a daily practice. James tells you what a person is like who says, "I love God," and then proceeds to act the direct opposite. "For if anyone is a hearer of the word and not a doer, he is like a man who looks at his natural face in a mirror; for once he has looked at himself and gone away, he has immediately forgotten what kind of person he was" (James 1:23–24, NASB).

Romans 6:12 says we should not let sin reign in our mortal body. That's what she's doing. So, you obviously are dealing with someone who says I'm a Christian but lives like a non-Christian, and I think their faith is suspect until they repent of their sins and give evidence of being born again.

Q: *I thought Christians were supposed to be loving. Why do some of them think it's okay to argue?*

When we see idolatry, we are supposed to be provoked. When we see evil, we are supposed to get incensed about it. If you can calmly walk through this upholstered cesspool of earth; if you can see evil, filth, degeneracy, and hear vile language; if you can see the corruption of the media and the perversion of the gospel; if you can see the multiple forms of idolatry—the worship of things and of the creation more than the Creator; if you can see this today and you are not provoked about it, then you are not in touch with God the Holy Spirit.

The Holy Spirit is provoked by evil, and He stirs up the Church so that we may do something about it. Christianity is not passive. Christianity is vigorously active.

Paul, a Hebrew of the Hebrews, blameless, trained under Gamaliel, with his PhD at the University of Damascus, stands in Athens. He looks around and sees idolatry, and he gets angry in his spiritual nature. Notice, the Scripture says he did something about it. He went out to try and reason with them.

Do you know what happens to people today when the Holy Spirit stirs them up? They turn on their television sets and skip prayer meeting. Am I right? I'm afraid that too often, it's true. But if you really are in the will of God, do you know what happens to you when the Holy Spirit provokes you? You go out and you do something about it. Paul went out and he argued.

We have people today who say, "Christians aren't supposed to argue. We're supposed to love." Gush, gush, gush. Let me ask you something. Do you think that argument for the truth excludes love? Love became flesh in Jesus Christ, and when love ran into the Pharisees, the Sadducees, the Herodians, and the Scribes, love argued with them.

Incarnate love has to tell the truth. If someone is dying, do you go to their hospital bed and "love" them so much you never tell them they're going to die in their sins? They are forever lost if you don't. What is love? Love is telling the truth.

Paul did not pick arguments. He went out and he witnessed for Jesus Christ, and when people argued with him, he answered them. Christians are supposed to give answers to the world. We are not supposed to go about looking for arguments, but we must love people so much that we are willing to argue for the truth.

Q: *How can I be a good and faithful servant?*

God gave mankind the capacity to do all of the above things, but the good and faithful servant is the one who invests the talents that God has given and does indeed become a servant to mankind. If the parable of the Good Samaritan means anything, it means that my neighbor is the person who needs me. The command is this: I should love my neighbor as I love myself.

It's obvious that if we, as professing believers, claim to have a relationship to Christ then we must invest the talents of God. Jesus is not talking about investing money in this passage, he's talking about investing life. We are good and faithful servants to the degree that we invest our lives, our fortunes, our abilities, and the talents God has given us for the service of our fellow man.

But the person who says, "I believe it" and the person who says, "I should do it," and doesn't do it, is the unfaithful servant.

He is the one who has all the appearance of godliness but disproves the reality of Christianity in his life, because he does not love his neighbor as himself. If we can see our neighbors—the disenfranchised and the poor—and it never touches us; if we are not going to share our substance with those who are in need, how then do we fulfill this parable?

The unprofitable servant is the one who, when people are hungry, doesn't feed them; when people are thirsty, he doesn't give them drink. Jesus is saying, "Don't you recognize that I'm giving you all of these opportunities to show your devotion to me? Don't you realize that in caring for the least of these—with whom I identify—you are ministering to me?"

We are supposed to invest the talents that God has given us. If we shut our minds and spirits to the needs of others, how then are we profitable servants? One thing is absolutely certain in this parable—God is telling you, if you really are His child, that you had better invest what He has made available to you: time, substance, money, concern, and compassion.

Q: *How do you tell someone about Jesus?*

I once had a friend who was the most gifted philosophy student at New York University. He scored in the upper one percentile of all philosophy students in the United States—an inconceivably brilliant mind. He used to needle me ruthlessly every chance he got because I was a Theist; I believed in God. We'd go at it time and time again.

One night, we were sitting in the cafeteria drinking coffee. I hated coffee at the time, and I was only drinking it as a means of testifying to him. So, I got a cup of coffee and a donut, and I sat there talking to him. I'll never forget it, it's as if it took place yesterday morning. His name was Kaye. We chatted back and forth for a couple of minutes, and he was needling me again. Finally, I said to him, "Kaye, tell me what you honestly think of Jesus of Nazareth."

He said, "Jesus of Nazareth was an extraordinary human being. He had fantastic insights into the minds of men and into their motives. I've read the New Testament and I'm very impressed with the person of Jesus." This, from a Jewish philosophy student!

"Good!" I said, "Do you think Jesus was essentially a truthful person?"

"Oh, I don't think there's any doubt about that at all," he replied.

"Would you say that Jesus was, perhaps, the greatest moralistic teacher you've ever read?"

"Oh, I don't think I'd doubt that for a minute, either. I've read all of them."

"I'm really glad to hear that," I said, "Now if you were me, knowing you as I do, hopping from bed to bed, boozing, swearing, telling dirty jokes, living just exactly the way you want to live. If you were me, would you listen to Jesus on the existence of God, or you?"

He looked at me for a minute, put his coffee cup down, and said, "If you put it that way, I think I'd listen to Jesus."

"There was never a moment of doubt," I said.

A few weeks later we were in class arguing vigorously again, with the Professor refereeing back and forth. All of a sudden, Kaye spouts off, "Now just a minute!" I thought, Oh boy, now I'm going to get it! But this time he said, "Martin and I are poles apart. We know our differences of opinion here. But you know, he does have a valid argument. His valid argument is on the person of Jesus. I don't hear anyone here saying they're equal with Jesus. Anybody here think they are? No? Well, that's Martin's position and until you are, shut up!"

Kaye and I became friends. We drank coffee regularly, and I gave it to him every chance I got. So, you see, the Lord uses little things—even a cup of coffee.

Q: *How does God manage to stand with the law and the spirit of life in Christ Jesus that sets us free from the law?*

By giving us a principle that we can live by—love. Romans 13:8, "Owe no man any thing, but to love one another: for he that loveth another hath fulfilled the law." When you try and fulfill the law in your daily life, you are a living disaster area and everyone knows it. Why? Because the perfection of the law condemns the imperfection of the sinner.

God says, "You shall not kill, steal, or commit adultery" but it is all condensed under this heading: "You shall love your neighbor as yourself." If you love the Lord your God with all your heart, soul, mind, and strength—and your neighbor as yourself—you fulfill the righteousness of God's law by applying the law of the spirit of life in Christ Jesus.

You can do it because you have been born again. You can walk in the light as He is in the light. You will abstain from coveting your neighbor's goods—but *not* because the law says you shall not covet. You will abstain from coveting your neighbor's goods because you love your neighbor as yourself and, therefore, you will not want to hurt him or anything that he has because you would not want to hurt yourself.

You will not take the name of the Lord your God in vain—but *not* because He said not to do it. You will abstain from blasphemy of the name of God because you love Him with all your heart, soul, mind, and strength. If you love someone that much, you will not blaspheme His name.

Q: *Can you shed some light on the meaning of Christ's words in Matthew 5:32?*

In this passage, Jesus said, "I say to you that everyone who divorces his wife, except for the reason of sexual immorality, makes her commit adultery; and whoever marries a divorced woman commits adultery."

The first part of the sentence says that everyone who divorces his wife, except for the cause of immorality, makes her commit adultery. This means that there is divorce on the grounds of sexual immorality. Whoever marries a divorced woman, commits adultery. If that woman is divorced from her husband other than on legitimate grounds, then she's involved in adultery. So, a legitimate ground for divorce would be sexual immorality.

Q: *What did Jesus mean in Matthew 15:5–6?*

Let's take a look back at the beginning of the chapter:

> Then some Pharisees and scribes came to Jesus from Jerusalem, saying, "Why do Your disciples transgress the tradition of the elders? For they do not wash their hands when they eat bread." And He answered and said to them, "And why do you yourselves transgress the commandment of God for the sake of your tradition?" (15:1–3, NASB)

In other words, He's answering them because they're charging His disciples with a sin. Now He goes on to charge them:

> "For God said, 'HONOR YOUR FATHER AND MOTHER,' and, 'HE WHO SPEAKS EVIL OF FATHER OR MOTHER IS TO BE PUT TO DEATH.' But you say, 'Whoever says to his father or mother, "Whatever I have that would help you has been given to God," he is not to honor his father or his mother.' And by this you invalidated the word of God for the sake of your tradition. You hypocrites, rightly did Isaiah prophesy of you:
>
> 'This people honors Me with their lips,
> But their heart is far away from Me.
> 'But in vain do they worship Me,
> Teaching as doctrines the precepts of men.'"
>
> (Matt. 15:4–9, NASB)

What Jesus is saying here is that the Pharisees said, "Yes, God did say, 'Honor your father and mother,' but when they get old (and need your financial support), then you can dishonor them." They were in reality putting tradition in place of Scripture.

The "precepts of men" was that you can say, "honor your father and mother, but do what you want to your parents." When you transgress the law of God (in not honoring your parents), you can just say, "Well, after all, everything I have (that would have supported you in your old age) has actually been given to God." They're trying to use God as an excuse for their sin, and He said you can't do that. You are invalidating the Word of God by using your tradition of interpretation.

It's human beings squirming their way out of obeying God. God said to honor your father and your mother. He who speaks evil of father or mother, let him be executed. But the Pharisees, scribes, and Sadducees allowed someone to *not* honor his father and his mother, by advising them to tell their parents, "Any funds I could use for parental support is now a gift to God, so I don't have to honor you anymore." Jesus said that invalidates the Word of God for the sake of Jewish tradition.

Q: ***A friend of mine says she is Christian. She believes Jesus is God but doesn't believe in hell or in the Bible as the Word of God. She also believes in universal salvation and the goodness of man's nature. Can I challenge her claim to being a Christian?***

You most certainly can, because she's denying good, solid biblical theology. It's possible the lady is a Christian who got sucked into some cult, though, and has picked up all these crazy doctrines and somehow thinks that this is Christianity.

If that's the case, you've got to spend time trying to find out if she is truly born again because people can say some pretty screwy things and still be Christians. If you doubt it, read your church history. You will find some people there saying utterly incredible things, yet there is quite a bit of evidence that they were born again.

Q: *According to the Bible, is there ever a time for revenge?*

Yes! There is a time for revenge according to the Bible. Are you ready—sharpening up your claws and fangs? Here it is: "Vengeance is mine. I will repay, says the Lord" (Deut. 32:25). That means keep your hands to yourself (rough translation). The Lord is going to bring perfect justice.

Incidentally, the word vengeance is a mistranslation. In the Greek, it reads "complete justice." God doesn't take vengeance as you and I think of taking it—we may think of getting even but God gives perfect justice. You get what you deserve, and that's far worse than human revenge. Take my word for it. According to Scripture, the lake of fire is what unregenerate demons and men deserve. That's far worse than any revenge you could ever take on this earth. So trust in the Lord—perfect justice is mine, I will repay, says the Lord.

Q: *If someone has caused you much harm financially and the loss of loved ones' affections, and you are sure this person defrauded the state too, should you report him or her?*

No, what you're doing is reporting someone for dishonesty and then waiting for the state to give you vengeance. You're making the state your agent of revenge. If you had nothing against that person, and you knew they were consistently breaking the law, there would be nothing wrong with bringing that to the attention of the authorities. But to bring in the authorities in order to get even with that person is the wrong motivation, and therefore fundamentally wrong in the eyes of God.

Now you could say, "well I'm just turning them in because they're dishonest." As long as you can justify that before the Lord, fine, but after telling me what they've done to you, I have a sneaking suspicion it would be more than a quest for honesty. I don't think I would do that.

Q: ***I have a question concerning how a Christian should handle their finances. We are a young couple who would like to establish credit but we're told we can't get credit because we don't have any credit. It seems if you are frugal with your money, the creditors reject you. If you owe everyone in town, then they accept you. Can you give us some good advice?***

Yes, avoid credit like the plague because credit is a trap. You get into it, and constantly feed your habit, and pretty soon it gets control of you. That being said, in our culture it is important to have a credit rating, so go to your local bank where you have your deposits and get into a Visa or Mastercard so you will have bank status in the community. If you've got that, you're safe and you can get that easily if you have an account in a bank and a good job.

Q: ***I brought someone with me this morning, but I told him he doesn't need to give anything in the offering. Do you agree?***

If you're a believer in the Lord Jesus Christ, we ask you to give generously to the class because in doing so, you are telling the Newport Mesa Christian Center that you believe in this Bible teaching ministry. Their only way of really knowing this is by our support. So if the Lord has prospered you, please give generously.

If you're not a believer in Christ, keep the money. Nobody's trying to get anything from you. We'd much rather give you something that is far more important. "The wages of sin is death but the gift of God is eternal life through Jesus Christ Our Lord" (Rom. 6:23). That's the gift the church wishes to give you.

Q: *Some people say we're not obligated to give a percentage of our money to God—just whatever we feel like giving.*

If you're a Christian, no one has to tell you to give generously to support the Lord's work. I use the word "generously" because we live in a selfish age, and human nature is deceitful and terribly selfish. Just stop and think about all the money that we spend as individuals for things in life—things that make us physically comfortable. We don't think anything at all about going out to a restaurant, or to some place for entertainment, and spending a good amount of money. It seems like we can always find a buck for something to take the tension off us so we can relax and enjoy ourselves. (Of course, I know *you're* not like that, but a lot of other people are, and the point is, we never stop and think.)

Then on Sunday morning, we drop a dollar or two in the collection plate, and we say to ourselves, "I'm discharging my obligation to the Lord."

Do you know what I think would be a good rule to follow in our Christian lives? Figure out how much money we spent during the week on luxuries, things we personally enjoy doing, and then match it for the Lord on Sunday—maybe with a dollar over to show him our concern. That would be consistent with our Christian testimony.

Q: *Offerings feel awkward at times, like people are trying to get money from us. What do you think?*

It's not for me, kid; it's for the work of God. You can't out-give Him. He's going to bless you, and if you've got it and you can give it, give generously. If you've got it and you won't give it, may the Lord reward you according to your works. And if you haven't got it at all, well, we'll pray for you, and you can pray for us. You're just as welcome as if you could pay the mortgage on the building.

Just don't play games with God. Don't try to equivocate. If you drop a couple of bucks in the offering and figure now you've done your job, you're a hypocrite. You haven't done your job. Your job is to give to the Lord generously and out of a heart filled with love. The most sensitive nerve in Christians' bodies, I'm convinced, is the pocketbook nerve. The minute you touch that nerve, people quiver all over the place. We've gotten that way because of the hucksters on television and radio, and the people who are always running around sticking their hands out. We get sick of it and say we're not going to give anything at all. That's throwing the baby out with the bathwater.

Be selective givers to the things you know are feeding your soul and your local church, and in this instance, your Bible class is feeding your soul. So that should be a prime directive. The Lord bless you, whether you can give or you can't.

Q: ***The Bible says that God joins a man and a woman together as one. I have a friend who believes that marriage is a tradition, and you don't have to be married to be joined as one in God's eyes. He also believes that fornication is going from woman to woman and not devoting yourself to one person. Could you please give me scriptures to show my friend that the Bible does believe that you must be married to be as one in God's eyes?***

First of all, in Romans 13:1–2 it says, "Let every person be in subjection to the governing authorities. For there is no authority except from God, and those which exist are established by God. Therefore he who resists authority has opposed the ordinance of God; and they who have opposed will receive condemnation upon themselves." Paul warns the Christians not to resist the bona fide requests of the authorities of your government because if you do, the man who carries the sword on his side doesn't have it there for fun and games. It's there for the purpose of executing judgment. That would correspond to the policeman and his gun on his hip today. So, the principle is very clear. You are married in the eyes of the state because the authorities desire that, and God says it is not contrary to His word.

As far as fornication is concerned, get your concordance out and look up the word fornication and you will have many references in the New Testament, particularly in Corinthians. Fornication is illicit sexual relations prior to marriage. The word *pornos*, where we get our word pornography or fornication from, refers to a whole spectrum of sexual sins ranging from fornication and adultery to bestiality and homosexuality. So, you are dealing with a broad range of sexual abuses. This is clearly taught in Scripture.

If you are cohabitating with somebody outside of marriage, God considers that fornication. Do not attempt to argue with him that you are confining your fornication to one person and therefore it's okay. Most of the people that follow this philosophy confine their fornication to one person at a time, and I have many times counseled young people in college and university level who come to me and say, "Well, we're living together but we love each other, and we can't afford to get married right now, so we consider ourselves married." This is not okay in God's eyes and nothing you can say will make it okay.

I get the same people back six months later and they've got another partner, and a year later they've got another partner, and each time God's going to okay their belief that they got married. This is fornication, and the Lord says to avoid it because whoever commits sexual sins, says Paul, sins against his or her own body. In other words, sexual sin is destructive to the physical body. Blessed in marriage but destructive outside of marriage. Recent statistics that I think are fascinating have shown that people who practiced immorality consistently in the areas of sexual sin are the people who inevitably have the most mental, emotional, and physical diseases and conflicts. They are literally trapped in guilt and they cannot escape from it. So they drink, take drugs, and keep up a hectic life in order to avoid facing the reality of their sin. The Scripture says it's no good. Inevitably, you have to pay the piper and they're dancing, and they will pay the piper.

So, if people give you that line of argument simply use the fornication references from the apostle Paul. The Lord Jesus said, "For from within, out of the heart of man, come evil thoughts, sexual immorality, theft, murder, adultery, coveting, wickedness, deceit, sensuality, envy, slander, pride, foolishness. All these evil things come from within, and they defile a person" (Mark 7:21–23 ESV). If Christ condemned it, the apostles condemned it, and Paul condemned it, then I think we ought to be willing to accept God's judgment on the subject.

Now you may say, "Well how can sexual sin before marriage actually affect a young, healthy, vibrant male or female? Well, God knew that the hepatitis virus lived in shrimp, lobsters, crab, and shellfish, and when they were taken out of the waters and not refrigerated, it was not safe. So, He said it was dangerous for the children of Israel to eat them and He forbid it. A lot of Jews said they tasted wonderful, and they died. If God knew the hepatitis virus was there, and He knew the trichinosis bacteria was in pork, then I think I'd trust Him if He tells you that sin of a sexual nature will produce results in your physical body, because it was not designed for that. The Scripture is explicit.

5

Defense of the Faith

Because of Dr. Martin's research in apologetics and the cults, he was often asked questions on how to deal with challenges to our faith, and especially those from specific groups. (Please note that some of the less-familiar groups discussed, while perhaps not as widespread as in Dr. Martin's day, are still operating.)

Q: *Someone told me that "The gospel is like a lion; all you have to do is turn it loose and it will defend itself." This doesn't sound right to me.*

The Bible tells us clearly in First Peter 3:15 to "Sanctify Christ as Lord in your hearts, always being ready to make a defense to everyone who asks you to give an account for the hope that is in you, yet with gentleness and reverence" (NASB). The work of Christian apologetics is not to apologize for Christianity, nor is it to attempt to destroy other people. We are summoned by God, not only to preach Jesus Christ as the Redeemer of mankind, but also to be prepared to give answers.

One of the reasons why the Christian church is weak and impotent today, and one of the reasons why the kingdom of the cults and the occult is growing, is because Christians think that all they have to do is tell people Jesus loves them, hand out a tract, do some normal personal work, and that's the end of our responsibility. This is not the truth, nor is it biblical. We are told by the apostle Paul to be "set for the defence of the gospel" (Phil. 1:16). This means that the gospel must be defended by the church.

The old saying that "The gospel is like a lion; all you have to do is turn it loose and it will defend itself" is not biblical. People are always using these illustrations and forgetting that Scripture says, "Earnestly contend for the faith which was once delivered unto the saints" (Jude 1:3).

Paul was absorbed with the idea of being a soldier of the cross, a follower of the Lamb. God requires that we become absorbed in exactly the same way. We must sanctify the Lord God in our hearts and be ready always to give to every man an answer. If we do this, we'll get the same effects the apostles got, we'll see the same results the church fathers' saw—the great apologists of the first five centuries—but we must do it. We can't pass the buck anywhere else. In the words of that immortal Baptist theologian, Harry Truman, "The buck stops here!" We must shoulder the responsibility and we must be bold.

Today, we've lapsed into the error of believing that somehow or other it is negative to defend the gospel. Nothing could be further from the truth. It is the most positive thing in the world to stand for Jesus Christ.

Q: *Please explain the difference between cults and the occult.*

A cult is a group of people gathered around someone's interpretation of the Bible. They always claim to agree with Christianity and end up denying the doctrines of the Trinity, the deity of Christ, and salvation by grace through the blood of the cross. You can always identify a cult immediately by those things. There are many other things that they deny too, but these will tell you almost instantly.

The occult is a series of practices rather than just one religion, and it can be in any religious group: astrology, witchcraft, or Satanism. Séances, Tarot cards, and fortune-telling are called tools of the occult—used to pique human curiosity and draw people into the occult. All of these things are the occult, which is practicing things God has forbidden in His Word and incorporating them into your religious practice and life. It is very dangerous and the dominion of demons.

Q: *What is the Scottish Rite of Freemasonry?*

The Scottish Rite Masonic Temple in Los Angeles is filled with demons and evil. If you go to it on Wilshire, you can see the evil all over the walls of the place. It reeks of evil. I know, I've been there. When I walked into the place, I felt horrible and I just wanted to get out of it as fast as possible. The only other places where I felt that kind of evil were in India at the temple of Kali, the goddess of death and destruction, and outside the Mormon Temple in Salt Lake City, Utah. I felt it there, believe me.

Q: *If on Judgment Day, God tells you the Mormons are right and you are wrong, would you then debate with God?*

I tried debating God on a number of occasions, and it was very unfruitful. God always seems to be three or four lightyears ahead of me, so I've given that up.

God cannot endorse Mormon theology without denying Himself. It's as clear as that. He says, "I am the eternal God. Apart from me, there isn't anyone else" (Isa. 45:5, ESV).

When I get to heaven, if God says, "There are millions of us [gods]," then I will know that I am not dealing with the God of the Bible. If I have to go into the lake of fire, it will be God who has lost His righteousness, not Walter Martin, because I believed what He said in His Word. So, there is no possibility that the Mormons can be correct, because they're polytheists, and there's only one God. God said so, I believe Him, and I have been delivered from the lake of fire because of the grace of the Lord Jesus Christ. I belong there and so do you. It's not a matter of opinion; it's a matter of what God said in His Word.

Q: *Is there a biblical viewpoint on hypnotism?*

The Bible says nothing on the subject of hypnotism. Some people have said that in Deuteronomy 18, a person who was a charmer was a hypnotist. But that's pure theory. Nobody knows.

Hypnotism can be a valuable tool in the right hands, and it can be a dangerous thing in the wrong hands.

Q: *Did purgatory originate from the Scriptures?*

Purgatory doesn't exist as a biblical doctrine. There isn't one single verse in the Bible that even inferentially suggests purgatory. Actually, purgatory developed at least 400 years after the apostolic age, and it was the result of a theological dilemma. According to theologians at that time, there were some people not good enough to go to heaven and not bad enough to go to hell. So, what did you do with those people?

Since the church had moved into a "works" perspective at that time, they began to think there must be some way we can deal with these people, and they originated the concept of a purging place. That's where the word purgatory comes from—it means "to purge away sin by suffering." The soul was then purified and it could enter heaven.

It is a pure rationalization, some three to four hundred years after the New Testament canon was closed. It was not apostolic doctrine.

Q: *How would you witness to very devout Catholics who insist on believing in purgatory?*

I would simply ask them to produce some text from the Bible that teaches it. Secondly, I would point out that the person who is born again enters immediately upon death into the presence of the Lord (2 Cor. 5:8), while the person who is not born again is kept under punishment until the day of judgment (2 Pet. 2:9). So, there's very little doubt about the problem once you see that there is heaven and there is hell, and nothing in between.

Q: ***A friend found out that her husband had some secret things underneath their bed related to the Masonic Temple. Apparently, he's been acting a little strange lately and doing all kinds of ritualistic types of things, and she didn't know anything about it.***

First of all, you can be a Mason and a Christian. I don't see how you can do it in good conscience, but nevertheless, you can be a Mason and a Christian. The oaths are contrary to the word of God (Matt. 5), but she does not need to fear these oaths. Some of them are pretty scary, but their so-called secrets have been known for a long time.

If they're both professing Christians, she certainly shouldn't divorce her husband because he's a Mason. She should witness to him and try to show him that Masonry is opposed to many of the basic foundations of the gospel, and then pray and ask the Lord to take it away from him. But belonging to the Masons is not grounds for divorce.

I would classify Freemasonry as a non-Christian cult because they do not believe in the deity of Jesus Christ. They reject the Christian doctrine of the Trinity and they do not believe that the salvation of the cross is sufficient to save from sin. Your own works have to be added to this. Masonry involves a great many pagan ideas, leaders and gods. Therefore, I don't think we should become involved with it at all.

Q: ***How do you know that Christianity is the true religion?***

I know Christianity is the true religion because the Scripture has been validated in my mind beyond a question of a doubt. Jesus

Christ is the centerpiece of the Scriptures and I accept the testimony concerning Him.

In addition to this, I had an existential encounter with Jesus Christ where I met Him. I know from archaeology. I know from history. I know from the validity of the text of Scripture. I know from the person of our Lord. I know from the Holy Spirit, and I know from personal experience. Those are very good reasons why.

You see, the difference between the rest of the religious leaders of the world and Jesus is this: They're dead. He's alive! The whole New Testament is based on the fact that He is risen. If He didn't rise from the dead as He said He would, no one would have believed in Him. They would have said He was a false prophet.

Do you remember what the Jews said when Jesus was dead on the cross? They wanted to put a watch on the tomb because the deceiver said He would return in three days. Pilate gave them their watch. They sealed the tomb with a Roman seal (Matt. 27:63–66). The soldiers were there—and the angel of the Lord rolled away the stone—and Jesus Christ wasn't there. They never recovered from the initial impact of that shock almost two thousand years ago. They're still trying to babble their way out of it, but they're not going to do it.

He's alive! I know because I pray for people week after week in the name of Jesus Christ, and they're healed. Dead saviors don't heal anyone.

Q: *What is happening with Christian Science?*

Christian Science is a dying cult. Their membership is disintegrating. The power of the Christian Science church, except for its great wealth, is in a very serious state of decay. I don't think it's necessary to flog a dying horse.

Christian Science is derived directly from Hinduism and its basic principle is just bankrupt. It teaches you that it is not necessary to believe in the cross as the only way of salvation. A person who says there's no life, truth, intelligence, or substance in matter but all is infinite mind (and its infinite manifestation for God is all in all) should be taken to Dachau or Auschwitz to get a good long look at the early pictures of six million corpses the Germans piled up. They should look at them eye to eye and nose to nose, and be asked: *Did they die?* If the answer is yes, then matter dies, and if it dies, matter exists. If it exists, the founder of Christian Science, Mrs. Eddy, lied. I don't think you have to go too far to point out that she lied. She denied that Jesus was the Christ, and that is the doctrine of the antichrist.

Q: *What do you mean by deprogramming people?*

By deprogramming, I don't mean a form of brainwashing. I mean answering people's questions, giving them reasonable alternatives, and showing them where they were misled. It is not a psychological process of pounding something into their heads. It is simply using the Word of God as the sword of the spirit, and Christian compassion to try to reach people. God will open their eyes if we are faithful.

Q: *I have a friend in Arizona who is a follower of William Branham. What can you tell me about Branham?*

He started out as a Pentecostal evangelist and ended up a heretic. I believe the Lord removed him from the earth by sovereign grace just so his early ministry of preaching the gospel wouldn't be destroyed, but he ended up teaching a false view of the Trinity and a number of other things. I believe God took him because God will sometimes destroy our bodies to save our souls (1 Cor. 5:5). If you fool around with God long enough, if you start messing up your Christian life and messing up the lives of other people, then you're not going to get away with it.

He has done this and He'll do it again. He told the apostle Paul, "Deliver such a one unto Satan for the destruction of the flesh, that the spirit may be saved in the day of the Lord Jesus." What does that mean? It means you've had it. He ends it by saying that your spirit may be saved at the day of the Lord Jesus. It's destroying the body to save the soul. That's love. Thank God that He loves us that much.

Q: Is First John 5:7 missing from all major manuscripts of the New Testament? [It is, except in the King James Bible.] Should we therefore not use it when witnessing to those who do not hold to the doctrine of the Trinity?

I wouldn't quote First John 5:7, because it's not in the best manuscripts of the New Testament. It appears in some manuscripts of the fifth century, but it does not exist in the major Greek manuscripts like the Sinaiticus or Codex Vaticanus (B) and Septuagint. Therefore, you should not quote it.

The King James Bible had it because it was based upon a manuscript that was not as good as the text we have now. Circle First John 5:7; it's called an interpolation. It's stating the truth, but it is not what John wrote. The King James Bible is not an infallible text. No translation is an infallible text. We have an accurate reproduction of an infallible text, but we don't have every detail of it and if we think we do, we're kidding ourselves. We have 90% of the New Testament as originally given and 95% of the Old Testament as originally given. But to argue that you've got every answer to every problem at the present moment is foolish.

I'll tell you one thing, it's breathtakingly accurate everywhere and nothing alters in reference to our salvation or the accuracy of what God wants to communicate. The translations can mislead you, particularly if they're based upon manuscripts that are not as early as the ones we have now.

I preach out of the King James Bible because I love it. There's never been a more developed masterpiece in the English language than the King James Bible, but it needs correction at various points with new information. That's one of the corrections that's needed. Of course, some people get very upset. I got a letter from a fellow not too long ago. It was one page long condemning me because I challenged the absolute authority of the King James Bible. After I read it, I could only think of one sentence he wrote: "If it's good enough for the apostle Paul, it's good enough for me." He thought that Paul wrote the text in King James English.

It's a good translation, amazingly good for the time, but it's not the best text. That's all. You should compare it to modern translations.

Q: *My mother has been going to the Church of Religious Science, and I was wondering is that a cult?*

Definitely. The Church of Religious Science is the cult of the science of mind founded by Ernest Holmes in 1926 in Los Angeles. It's very similar to Unity School of Christianity, Christian Science, and Metaphysics. It denies the deity of Jesus Christ, the doctrine of the Holy Trinity, and the virgin birth. It denies the atonement of the cross as the means of salvation and the bodily resurrection of the Lord Jesus. It is a very dangerous non-Christian cult.

Q: *Is it true that cults tend to have very strong authority figures in their leadership, with lot of control?*

Yes, that's a fairly common characteristic of many cultic structures but you have to be careful, here. In the Christian church, there has to be authority vested in the clergy and in their teaching ministry, otherwise you have anarchy. So just because someone is authoritarian, and someone may have strong commitments and positions, doesn't mean that they're a cult leader.

What really makes a cult is a combination of things, not just one characteristic. For example, if a church member wanted to take another job, and they had to get permission from their leader to do it, or if they wanted to buy a new car or a new house, and permission was required from the leadership, that would be an example of going too far in authoritarian rule in the church.

Q: ***I know someone who is into this positive confession stuff, and lately she just can't get over saying that we have the mind of Christ, that Christ was a Creator and we can create, too. When it comes to any decision, she just keeps saying you have the mind of Christ. I am just wondering if you could tell me what the mind of Christ is, as far as a believer goes?***

Yes, they ignore the context of the mind of Christ.

> Let this mind be in you, which was also in Christ Jesus: Who, being in the form of God, thought it not robbery to be equal with God: But made himself of no reputation, and took upon him the form of a servant, and was made in the likeness of men: And being found in fashion as a man, he humbled himself, and became obedient unto death, even the death of the cross (Phil. 2:5–8).

That is the mind of Christ—the total willingness to be in subjection to the will of God the Father.

Jesus was at all times subject to the Father, and He said He did only those things that pleased Him. The mind of Christ is interpreted for you by the apostle Paul in Philippians 2, and it's a mind of humility. It's a mind of subjection. The Greek word is literally "disposition." Let this disposition or attitude be in you that existed in Jesus Christ. Positive confession is certainly not representing Christ's attitude when they tell you that you can do everything Christ can do, because nowhere in the Bible does it say that at all.

Q: ***What is* Dianetics?**

Dianetics is a book by L. Ron Hubbard, related to a very dangerous non-Christian cult called Scientology.

Q: ***Couldn't Scientology be charged with false and deceptive advertising since their flock is sucked in with self-help Dianetics on television, and once in, they spring Scientology on the softened-up group?***

Well, you'd never be able to prove it, but that's precisely what they do. *Dianetics* is L. Ron Hubbard's book, and it leads you right into Scientology.

Q: ***Did the doctrine of the Trinity come out of the Council of Nicaea?***

The Jehovah's Witnesses argument is that the Trinity doctrine came out of the Council of Nicaea. The truth is that it was enunciated in the second century by Tertullian, a Latin Church Father around the year 174, which indicates that they haven't done their homework.

The Council of Nicaea wasn't a trinitarian conference at all. It was a council to deal with the Arian heresy in the church that denied the deity of Christ, so they haven't done their homework a second time.

Don't pay too much attention to the Watchtower on the Trinity. They are terribly ignorant of church history and of biblical theology, so you've got to approach them patiently. Take the time to get your ammunition together and then talk with them.

Q: ***What is it with philosophy? It's all so confusing and my professor doesn't seem very rational or logical.***

I took my B.A. in Philosophy, and my master's degree under Dr. Sidney Hook at New York University. Dr. Hook was a disciple of John Dewey, the greatest enemy of Christianity we've had in the last hundred years here in the US. I know all the reasons why I should be an agnostic, and all the reasons why I should be an atheist—and they're all a crock of garbage! They're just a cover-up for your sins.

Let me show you how far they'll go. Dr. Hook was one of the most brilliant philosophers in the world. I took specific notes in his class. One day Dr. Hook was asked, "What would you accept as absolute proof of the existence of God? How do you deal with the problem of God yourself, personally?"

Dr. Hook answered—in my class, in my hearing, with my eyes fastened on him—"If I were to die and wake up in the presence of Jehovah, I would be able to give Him logically consistent arguments as to why I did not accept His existence when I was on the earth." That's a direct quote!

So yours truly—old trouble-maker—raised his hand and said, "Dr. Hook, *sir*" (he was a formidable teacher), "wouldn't the fact that you woke up and He was there destroy all your logical arguments?"

"Ah, well," he answered, "you have to understand that I live essentially by the laws of formal logic. I believe in logic as a means of truth."

I said, "That isn't the point. The point is that if you wake up and He's there, you were wrong. All your logic is wrong. The fact that He's there proves it." Well, he rambled off on something else and I never got an answer.

What kind of ego is it that thinks it can wake up in the presence of an infinite intellect—who knows all arguments as conclusions—and discuss logic? He knows everything as a basic premise before you even open your mouth! He knows what it is, what you're going to say and where you're going with it. How could you wake up in His presence and say, "The reason I didn't believe in you is logically demonstrable." God would say, "Fascinating.

I'm here, aren't I? You're here, aren't you? One of us isn't thinking straight and it certainly isn't Me!"

I'll tell you something about the philosophers that they don't normally discuss. I learned this after about 10 years of study in the field. Here it is, ready? A great secret truth: all schools of philosophy, almost without exception, refute their predecessors so that as each new school arises, the next school refutes it. They just keep going on and on in this everlasting cycle of drivel, refuting each other.

They never built a hospital; they never built an old age home. They made no contributions whatever to the social welfare of mankind. They are parasitical individuals who live off the festering carcass of education and unbelief. That's exactly what they are. They argue all the time in their own defense. They're always defending their own sins.

Q: ***Our family has been concerned about the faith teaching of Kenneth Copeland and other ministries. They say you can stand on anything that's in the Word of God and it will come to pass. I was wondering how that teaching holds up scripturally?***

It doesn't hold up scripturally at all. It's not a Christian teaching. It has not been the position of the Christian church from its earliest days. It is a revival of an ancient Pentecostal heresy of the last 100 years or so. It didn't work in the early 1900s; it didn't work in the 1920s; it flopped in the '30s; it fell apart in the '40s, and was resurrected in the '70s.

Q: ***John 3:5 says except a man be born of water and the spirit he cannot enter the kingdom of God. Does this mean that water baptism is essential to salvation? The Church of Christ says so.***

The doctrine of baptism for salvation is an old one but John 3:5 isn't teaching it. Jesus said, "Truly, truly, I say to you, unless one is born of water and the Spirit, he cannot enter into the kingdom of God." There was no Christian baptism when Jesus uttered that statement. It was only the baptism of John, and that was the baptism unto repentance. So, all Jesus was saying was except a man be born of water and repent of his sins as John is baptizing and received the Holy Spirit, which was not yet given, he could not enter the kingdom of God. He was talking about the Christian dispensation that was to come—it had not yet begun. It began at the cross on Pentecost, so you are not getting baptism as a means of salvation in John 3:5.

***Q:* A man came to my door from the Church of Christ and said you weren't saved unless you were in the Church of Christ. He said that all my Bible reading and talking to him was in vain; that reading the Bible can only be understood if you're a member of the Church of Christ or if they come to your door.**

The Church of Christ is less than a hundred years old and I'm wondering what the Christian Church did without them for almost nineteen centuries. Think of it—we were in darkness until the Church of Christ arrived on the scene!

I have offered to debate a recognized representative of the Church of Christ numerous times on their views on baptism and other issues. It's been difficult getting them to come out of the woodwork. They'll send me a local pastor, but you can debate local pastors from now until purgatory freezes over, and never get to the Church of Christ. What you want to do is debate a representative of the denomination, which I offered to do with the United Pentecostal Church too. This is the fifth week that we are still waiting for their response, so we expect that the Church of Christ won't do it, either.

Paul says in First Corinthians 1:17 that Christ did not send him to baptize, but to preach the gospel. Baptism is not the gospel. Baptism is a sacrament of the church, not the gospel.

The gospel is that Christ died for our sins according to the Scriptures. He rose again on the third day. We are to believe that He is God's Son, that He died for our sins, and that He rose from the dead. That is the gospel.

If you have any doubt about it, read First Corinthians 15:1–4: "Brethren, I declare unto you the gospel," that Christ was delivered to death for our offenses and raised to life for our justification. It's very simple, so we should not let the Church of Christ disturb us. There are lots of loonies around the landscape, and what we must do is love them and pray for them. A lot of them have been taken out of Christian churches and are believers, but very confused believers.

The Church of Christ is a good example of majoring on the minors and confusing everyone. It's an imbalance—like the United Pentecostal Church. They talk about the gospel and about salvation, but when you start asking questions, they have a totally different concept of the Trinity. It's a totally different concept of Christ, and they tell you that you must speak in tongues in order to be saved. The United Pentecostal Church has always been considered heretical—by both Pentecostals and evangelicals.

Q: *I believe a good percentage of the followers of Witness Lee and the Local Church are truly born again. What scriptures do you show them to reveal to them that Mr. Lee is not adhering to the Word of God?*

I preached a message on Witness Lee and the Local Church[1] before almost 4,000 people. The people of the Local Church came that night and we gave them a question-and-answer period. It's all recorded on an hour-and-a-half tape. Witness Lee

1 The Local Church is the name of the church attended by the followers of Witness Lee.

never refuted that lecture, but he's heretical on the Trinity. He says the Father became the Son, the Son became the Spirit, and the Spirit in the end becomes the church. This is modalistic existentialism in theology, and it's erroneous because the Father never became the Son. If you want proof of that, simply read the concept that Christ had of this in John 10:30: "I and my Father are one." I and my Father—two persons—we are in union. In Matthew 28:19, Jesus taught His disciples to baptize people in the name of the Father, Son, and Holy Spirit. They ignore these passages.

Q: *Please define what constitutes a cult and why.*

The dictionary gives you four meanings for the word cult. They are all accurate, but a cult must be defined functionally. What is a cult? It's a group of people gathered around someone's interpretation of the Bible. It always claims to be harmonious with Christianity, but will always deny that Jesus Christ is God in human flesh. It always denies salvation by grace alone and the Christian doctrine of the Trinity. You can be absolutely certain it's a cult by applying those three things—you'll know that you're dealing with a non-Christian cult.

Q: *Why do you consider the United Pentecostal Church a cult?*

I consider them a cult—and I have stated this publicly many times on the air and on television—because they teach doctrines that are definitely opposed to historic Christianity. They teach that you must speak in tongues to be saved, which the church has never taught. They teach that Jesus is not part of a Trinity: Father, Son, and Holy Spirit. That is not Christian theology. They are considered a cult because of these views, and because they constantly attack the Christian church.

Q: *A judge in Salt Lake City wants the government to explain why they don't permit polygamy.*

I think this is a great idea. It should go into the courts and we should all discuss polygamy, particularly since there are still Mormons who practice it. We know where they are and so does the Mormon church, and they excommunicated them even though they're absolutely correct. Mormonism taught polygamy, so did Joseph Smith and Brigham Young, and they practiced it. If they're going to be consistent they should follow their leaders.

Q: *What exactly is Kabbalah? What is its history?*

It is pagan or cultic Judaism—occultism mixed with Judaism that blasphemes the God of Israel. It is not valid. It is evil, and it is condemned and cursed by God.

Q: *I had a Mormon missionary tell me the Bible wasn't complete. I told him about Revelation 22:18–19. I guess that wasn't the thing to say; he told me that Revelation was written before the Bible was completed. What is a good reply to this comment?*

He's wrong. The Book of Revelation was the last book. It was written by John. He outlived everybody, so it was the last book. The principle is true: if you add to the Word of God, God will add to you judgment. If you take away from His Word, God will take away your portion from immortality. The argument that the Bible is incomplete is an old one, not based upon the facts of Scripture or the teachings of the apostles.

Q: *How wealthy is the Hare Krishna cult?*

Their wealth is considerable. They can pay the $9.5 million lawsuit against them, but I don't think it will go through. I think some soft-headed clod up the line is going to reduce the judgment and by the time it gets to the Supreme Court, if it ever goes that far, they'll probably get rid of the whole thing.[2]

Q: *Please comment on the door-to-door Church of Christ people who say no one is saved unless they are baptized in their church. This man at my door went on and on with countless scriptures to support his claims. He said every church other than his church is evil, and he keeps coming to my house to "save my soul," which can only be done by him and his church. How can we remedy this?*

No, Scripture doesn't support his claims. They just quote scriptures out of context and in error to convince you to listen. If you're really having trouble with this man, you should ask your pastor to come over; perhaps your pastor can even greet this man at your door. Once he encounters the pastor, he will not be back again.

This is typical theological error, and you shouldn't pay any attention to it. The Church of Christ promulgates this kind of thing, and they are very divisive. There are people in there that are born again, but whatever divides the body of Christ is not of the Holy Spirit. The Spirit's ministry is to bring the church together, to unify us in the Lord Jesus Christ.

If you've got somebody dividing the body using classical biblical doctrines such as the deity of Christ, the virgin birth, the nature of God, or salvation by grace, then you know that you are dealing with a cultic operation. There are Christian cults and there are non-Christian cults, and the Church of Christ qualifies as a Christian cult because they don't spend a lot of their time preaching the gospel—they spend a lot of their time chewing up the church. I consider many of their practices very cultic, and I've offered to

2 The $9.5 million class-action lawsuit against the International Society of Krishna Consciousness for child abuse in their temples and schools was settled in 2005, and resulted in the society declaring bankruptcy.

debate bona fide representatives of the Church of Christ, but it's very difficult to get somebody designated by the denomination.

Q: *Could you explain a little bit about how the Christian is to consider the work of Pseudo-Dionysius, especially his letters to Timothy?*

What you have with these writings is a lot of material that is apocryphal, pseudepigraphical or just outright counterfeit material, like *The Aquarian Gospel* and things of this nature. You shouldn't bother with it because it was examined a long time ago and found to be absolutely irrelevant, meaningless, and contrary to Scripture.

Think of a book that's published and advertised in the National Inquirer or some other rag sheet and it says, "The Lost Books of the Bible: What the Church Has Been Hiding From You. Send in your $7.95 and find out what you've been missing." They really should say, "Send in your $7.95, suckers, and buy the garbage that the church rejected almost 2,000 years ago." The Jews also rejected it, so that's all there is to it.

This is phony stuff that was tested and rejected, so if you want to be a sucker for that kind of thing, go ahead. PT Barnum said, "There's a sucker born every minute," and he ought to know. All he'd need to do today is look over the evangelical and charismatic world, and he could find them by the barrels. There are people willing to give their money to support anyone, and to promulgate any doctrine. They never take their Bible and put the Word of God to the test. They never test the lives of the people teaching them to find out if they line up with Scripture.

Is the person a true prophet or a false prophet? Remember that false prophets speak in Jesus' name, and cast out demons in Jesus' name. The false prophets call Him Lord, and the false prophets preach in His name. Jesus said they even work miracles in His name. "And then will I profess unto them, I never knew you: depart from me, ye that work iniquity" (Matt. 7:21–23).

False prophets will do all of these things, so how can we know who is the true one and who is false? That's the job of teachers; that's what I do. That's the job of pastors; that's what they do. They are called to protect as well as to feed the sheep.

So many times the sheep don't like to hear it. You tell them, "This is false doctrine; that it is evil; you shouldn't go near it." But the sheep say, "They're such nice people. Look how they talk about Jesus and look at the miracles they do. They're such wonderful Christians." I get this all the time. I have people jumping on my case constantly because I'm pointing out false doctrine, but that's what I'm supposed to do. If you don't do it, if you don't have the guts to stand up for what you believe in, you are not much good to the church, really, because the church needs people with conviction.

Now, I will say one thing for my students, without fear of contradiction: they have minds of their own. I know, because they write me nasty letters from time to time and tell me where they disagree with me, or they send me questions and come up to talk with me.

Think; use your mind. That's what separates you from the animals. You have reason and logic; use them. If some guy comes down the pike on television and says everything is wonderful, look out!

Q: ***If a Hare Krishna or a Moonie (Unification Church) approaches you to sell you something, what is the best way to respond to them, other than to simply say you can't support something you don't believe in? Should we try to witness to them about Jesus? How can we rebuke them without appearing to have no concern for their souls?***

Yes, you should try to witness to them about Jesus. You don't need to rebuke them for coming to you. What you can do is tell them what Christ did for you, give them your testimony, and enter into a dialogue that answers their questions. If you do that, then you are witnessing effectively to them. Definitely witness to them; don't just turn them off by saying, "I don't support your work."

Q: *Have you heard of Bill Hayman, supposedly a prophet? He says he's positive confession all the way. What do you know about him?*

Not much, but if he's into positive confession all the way, I know one thing about him instantly: he's not a biblical scholar or a good student of the Bible. You can't absorb the doctrine of positive confession and really believe it if you know biblical theology. It's the direct opposite of biblical theology.

Positive confession says, "Name it and claim it," or "Blab it and grab it." But the Scripture says that if we ask anything including health and healing, and it be in accordance with His will, He hears us, and if He hears us, we know we have what we require (1 John 5:14–15). The big error of positive confession is that your faith is on the throne of the universe. You are telling God what to do.

As I've often said on the radio, it's extremely unsafe to discuss the existence of the deity in His presence. He doesn't like it and He doesn't like you telling Him what to do because He's not going to do it anyhow. He's going to do what He wants to do, so look out for that doctrine—it's widespread and it's splitting an awful lot of churches.

Q: *What do you know about Howard Ruff?*

He is a Mormon economist who appeared on the 700 Club—God only knows why. The Mormons love that, because any time a Mormon gets on a Christian program, they trumpet it all over the country. They say, "Walter Martin says we're a cult. Ed Decker says we're a cult, but we were on the 700 Club. We were on this Christian program." It gets thrown back in your face.

All I can say is that Christians make some awfully stupid mistakes, and what we ought to do is stop giving opportunities to the enemies of Jesus Christ. Howard Ruff and Jack Anderson (a Mormon newspaper columnist) went on the Christian Broadcasting Network. Both of them denied the Trinity and the deity of Christ. They made a bastard out of the Lord Jesus; they denied salvation by grace alone and added human works to it, something condemned by the book of Galatians. All of this these men believed and propagated; they tought heresy, and we put them on Christian programs and exposed them to the world. Do you think that's intelligent? I think that's a form of delusion and somebody should say something about it.

Q: ***Herbert Armstrong claims to teach the "real" gospel. How do you know which gospel is real and how do you enter into the kingdom of God?***

You know if Herbert's telling the truth by matching his idea of Jesus and salvation with the Bible's idea. The Bible says Jesus Christ is God the Son, Second Person of the Trinity. Herbert Armstrong says the Trinity is pagan; there is no Trinity, and you can become God as Jesus is God. That tells you immediately that he has another Jesus, a different spirit, and another gospel. You don't even have to be a biblical scholar. You can be an average layman or Sunday school student and know that if you're talking about another Jesus, you're not talking Christianity. Herbert Armstrong is a non-Christian cultist. That's how you know which is the gospel of the Kingdom.

Q: ***What are some scriptures that teach against the preexistence of the soul? Can a Christian hold to that doctrine? Please explain Jeremiah 1:5 about Jeremiah being sanctified before he was formed in the belly.***

Jeremiah 1:5 is simply saying what the Bible teaches throughout—namely, that known to God are all His works from the beginning of time. He saw us in Jesus Christ before time began. That does not mean we existed before time began. It means God saw us in His mind. That's all it means. So, when He talks about Jeremiah being sanctified, or Paul being called from his mother's womb, it doesn't mean that Paul or Jeremiah existed before. It means God knew them before time began and at the proper time, brought them into existence.

I dealt with the pre-existence of the soul in my book, *The Maze of Mormonism*, and I listed a number of texts and the refutation of the Mormon position. This is their doctrine, that you pre-existed with mommy and daddy God, grandmommy and granddaddy God, and with great-grandmommy and great-granddaddy God—ad infinitum, ad nauseam. They believe in many gods. They believe you can actually become one, and they believe the gods go on from all eternity.

It is clearly stated in Mormon theology, since the time of Brigham Young, that there never was a time when there were no gods. That's a lie. There never was a time when God did not exist, but there is only one God; everything else is satanic. So, obviously, you don't have to get too upset about the doctrine of pre-existence. It is not a biblical doctrine.

Q:* *What do you think about mainline churches that backed Reverend Moon in his tax fraud case? None of their support pretends to have any fondness for Moon. They all said there is no particular sympathy for the defendant in this case and no agreement with his faith is required to feel grave distress at the resulting breach of religious liberty.

That's garbage! Moon violated the tax laws of the United States, and I don't care if he's the pope. His religious position doesn't give him the right to violate the laws of the land. He is subject to the same laws. Read Romans 13—we are all subject to the law of the land. Paul says if you break the law, look out. Christian or no Christian, they're coming for you.

We do not need a lot of bleeding-heart liberals running all over the place telling us it's threatening our religious liberty. It is not. It's protecting the Constitution of the United States. It's not even touching our religious liberty. If the law says you are a crook, you ought to be in the slammer for it, no matter who you are.

Somebody might argue that's not very loving. It's very just, and whoever told you that justice was loving? Go up to Soledad Prison. I've been there—not as an inmate, but as a visitor. I'm happy to tell you there are a lot of people up there that confirm there is no love in justice at all.

This is what we face in dealing with God: If you don't want love, you can have justice. Mr. Moon got it. Frankly, I think he'll skip the country, and if I were in his shoes, that's what I would do if I'd exhausted everything else. I'd split because I wouldn't want to stay in the slammer. He's a multi-millionaire—he can go back to Korea and live like a king, and that's precisely what he will do. I think what we should do is send him out of the country. If he leaves the US, then close down his entire operation. That's the quickest way to deal with Mr. Moon.[3]

Q: *The Kubler-Ross books are being recommended by some local pastors. Is she a Christian? In one of her books is a chapter on Hinduism and Buddhist teachings on death which she says we can profit from. Please comment.*

No, she's not a Christian. Elisabeth Kubler-Ross is into the occult, and also into out-of-body experiences that take you right into the world of the occult. She is a psychiatrist and a medical doctor, but in this area, she is bananas. You are going to get yourself into some real trouble if you take her too seriously.

3 *Editor's note:* In 1982 Moon was convicted in the United States of filing false federal income tax returns and conspiracy. He was given an 18-month sentence and a $15,000 fine. Moon returned to South Korea and continued leading the Unification Church until his death in 2012.

Q: *Were you ever able to speak to Pat Boone who is supposedly one of the owners of TV channel 56 in Anaheim about the* Dianetics *and Mormon commercials on the station?*

I did not get to speak to him, but other people did. Apparently, he said he does not own the entire station, only part of it. I think he would like to divest himself of the station and his interest in it. He does not believe in *Dianetics*. He does not believe in Mormonism. He is not in sympathy with what they are doing, but he has no control over it. If he owned the station, it would be a different story, but he doesn't. He's no different than lots of people, Christians included, who own stock in companies that are not of a Christian nature; they still own the stock in the companies, even though they don't endorse what's going on. So, he finds himself in that category.[4]

Q: *A Jehovah's Witness used to use Acts 28:6 to justify their translation of John 1:1. How can I explain this problem, since there is no article preceding the word* theos *in either passage? Thanks.*

This has been answered in detail in my book, *The Kingdom of the Cults*, (Bethany House, 1965, 2019) and also in *Jehovah of the Watchtower* (Bethany House, 1974). They simply ignore the laws of Greek grammar at will. What they are talking about here is a violation of context. In Acts 28, the passage deals with pagans. Therefore, "a god" would be a proper rendition. In John 1, the context is dealing with Christ and the church, and with Israel's view of God. Therefore, it cannot be translated "a god" in Greek or by context, and no scholars agree with the Jehovah's Witnesses translation at this point. It's a phony translation.

---

4 *Editor's note:* Pat Boone and others in his investment group eventually divested themselves of the TV station. The station went on to broadcast classic TV shows and dropped its Christian programming.

Q: *Can a Christian with minimal witnessing experience talk intelligently and witness to a Saturday morning Jehovah's Witness?*

They can learn. I don't think you should send babies out to do a man's job, though. If you are ignorant of the Scriptures and have minimal experience in witnessing, you should study. "Study to shew thyself approved unto God, a workman that needeth not to be ashamed [or blush on Saturday morning before a Jehovah's Witness], rightly dividing the word of truth" (2 Tim. 2:15). I have four audio messages on how to witness to Jehovah's Witnesses; two with Bill Cetnar called "Dialogue on the Doorstep with Jehovah's Witnesses," and another two called "The Do's and Don'ts of Witnessing to the Cults." Get that material, go over it, and when they knock on your door next Saturday morning, open it and say, "Come right in, I've been waiting for you!" You won't have any problem after that, but you should not do it unless you are sufficiently informed.

Q: *Is this the way a Christian gains experience—through on-the-job training?*

Yes, I think you should get a little information first, and then you should get as much on-the-job training as you can.

Q: *Do you feel a person can be an expert on cults and the occult by knowing their doctrine well?*

Yes.

Q: *What do you think about Rabbi Kushner's book,* When Bad Things Happen to Good People*?*

We reviewed the book and it's not worth it. It postulates the idea of a finite God who really doesn't get involved in things. That is not the God of the Bible—He gets involved in everything.

Q: *Can you tell us about the Mormon who got saved on his deathbed after more than 30 years in the Mormon church?*

Yes—praise the Lord!

He had been a Mormon all of his life but he had some real misgivings about Mormonism. The doctor came into his room and told him he wasn't going to make it, so he knew he was dying and he wanted to be sure of where he was going. He started praying about it, and one day a Christian came in and gave him a copy of *The Maze of Mormonism*, and he immediately thought, *That's got to be an answer to prayer*. So, he read the book on his deathbed, and after he read it, he got his Bible out and compared it with his Bible, and he accepted Christ on his deathbed.

God healed him. He raised him up, and he's now witnessing all over Oregon. He called me on the radio to tell me about his salvation. He was praising the Lord! He said, "Thirty years in the Mormon church and God touched me, healed me, and saved me. I've got to be a witness." And that's exactly what he is.

Needless to say, it has disturbed considerable elements in the Mormon church in that area, so we can pray for him, because God has blessed him. That's a praise report you can really thank the Lord for.

Q: *Can you please comment on the subject of Scientology and L. Ron Hubbard?*

Scientology is a non-Christian cult that began with the publication of L. Ron Hubbard's book *Dianetics* back in 1950. Hubbard organized a church around his ideas and developed it into a multi-million-dollar operation. It's what we call an instant-analysis, mind-science cult. For specified amounts of money, they promise to "audit" you to find out what's going on inside your mind and your soul. They do this by having you hang on to two tin cans which are connected to a galvanometer-type device—an instrument that measures electronic current. Then they ask you questions. Your electrical impulses are recorded, and they tell you they are analyzing your engrams. What is an engram? It is a traumatic experience in your mind or your soul from a past reincarnation that is now the origin of your all your current troubles.

Scientology capitalizes first of all on gullibility. Running close behind that is sheer stupidity, and finally, it capitalizes on the terrible vacuum in the soul of man that is always looking for something spiritual but is unwilling to submit to the sovereignty and grace of God.

This is what you're up against, and Hubbard has made a great deal of money on it. It's a non-Christian cult that denies the Trinity, the deity of Christ, the blood atonement on the cross, and the resurrection of the Lord Jesus. Hubbard is a very dangerous man in his thinking. We ought to pray for those who are prisoners of this cultic system. Hubbard has no qualifications for what he does—no training in the areas of psychology or psychiatry. He's just a science fiction writer who made it big.

The horror is that it has destroyed the spiritual thinking process of so many people. I just received a very lovely letter from L. Ron Hubbard's son, who changed his name and recently tried to get his father declared dead or to make the Scientologists produce him to see if he was mentally competent. Hubbard had to finally come out under court pressure; he was still alive.

This guy is a born-again Christian who loves the Lord and prays for his father, but he came to my lectures in Carson City, Nevada, and was praising and thanking God for his conversion. He wanted to encourage me to go on doing what I was doing because it was so important that people find out that Scientology and the cults were counterfeit, and deadly to the human soul. That is the son of the founder of the Scientology cult—one of the most terribly influential groups running around loose today.

Q: *Please explain Matthew 5:39–41: "But I say unto you, That ye resist not evil: but whosoever shall smite thee on thy right cheek, turn to him the other also. And if any man will sue thee at the law, and take away thy coat, let him have thy cloak also. And whosoever shall compel thee to go a mile, go with him twain."*

Christ knew the customs of the Jews in social relations. When they became angry, they would shout at you. They would call down curses on you, and then the supreme insult in the Jewish culture was to pull the beard, spit in the eye, and slap the cheek. You can still see that in the Semitic world today. It's still there, so Jesus gave an illustration: He said, "Do you know how you are to act toward your fellow man? Let me show you. Even if it gets to the point where they pull the beard, spit in the eye and slap you on the cheek" (that was the supreme insult—a slap on the cheek) "you'll be willing to take the second blow, because it is a testimony to your willingness to leave the matter at the judgment seat of God rather than try to resolve it yourself."

Jesus knew there was something in the nature of man that causes anger and hatred to lash out. If you are willing to take someone's abuse, it will bring a grudging respect. Something happens—people change when these things occur. Jesus knew that. After all, He created the nature of man. Even though it was fallen, He knew this was true. That's what we're supposed to do in the normal activities of life. Take what comes—even abuse. Turn the other cheek. Even if it gets to the point where you get hit on one cheek, as in the Jewish culture, be willing to accept the second blow.

One minor footnote here: Jesus did not say it was wrong to defend yourself after the second blow. He didn't say you should stand there and get your brains beat out. He said be willing to take the insult, but if it gets to the place where you're going to have to preserve yourself, he told his disciples to sell their cloaks and purchase a sword, if necessary. So much for the alleged pacifism of the Lord Jesus Christ. I wish the pacifists would read this every once in a while to refresh their memories.

Q: *Do you believe in the power of prayer?*

I believe in the power of prayer. The Scripture says the effectual, fervent prayer of a righteous man avails much (James 5:16). Every person in this room this morning is as righteous as God Himself by faith in Jesus Christ, and therefore our prayers will be heard.

6

Satan, Demons, and Hell

Dr. Martin received many questions about Satan, evil, and "spiritual wickedness in high places" (Eph. 6:12). Here are his answers from Scripture.

Q: *What is the origin of evil?*

A choice was made in the angelic realm—Lucifer chose to rebel against God and to try to become like God. Evil came about in heaven and on earth as a result of choice.

Love comes from choice. God created the capacity to choose among angels and men or He would never have known love from them. Humans are neutral with the capacity of choice. We made a choice in Adam for evil.

God was willing to undergo all the pain and suffering of this situation because He could see the light at the end of the tunnel; He could see that there would be a great multitude of angels and men who would love Him and choose to love Him because of His great love for them. Somehow, He managed that love on the cross in the Lord Jesus Christ and it has redeemed us. The origin of evil is free choice. The origin of redemption is God's love reaching out to us so that we could choose to love Him because of Jesus Christ.

Q: *If God is good and if God is just, how do we explain the existence of evil?*

How do we explain the problem of pain and suffering? How do we come to grips with a world which quite obviously is dominated not by good, but by forces which are quite the opposite? I think the Christian has to wake up to the fact that this kind of problem can't be swept under the rug.

First of all, the term omnipotence has to be defined as quickly as possible. What do we mean when we talk about omnipotence? Well, in the Latin from which it comes it simply means "all-powerful." So when we say that God has as one of his primary attributes omnipotence, we are talking about all power being vested in God. It is extremely important at this juncture that you understand this: all power does not mean the capacity to do anything the person who possesses it chooses. Omnipotence means "all power," but not necessarily the capacity to do anything that you wish to do.

So let's face it for what it is: there are things that God, though omnipotent, cannot do. These are the things contrary to His revealed nature. The Scripture says, for instance, that it is impossible for God to lie (Heb. 6:18). It is impossible for God to do something in eternity and then contradict it in time. It is impossible for God to fail. God cannot countenance sin; He cannot, because He is holy. There are at least fourteen or fifteen things the Scripture tells us that God *cannot*—not *will not*, but *cannot*—do. There are limitations imposed by God's character—by His nature. So as we face the problem of evil, let's understand the definition of omnipotence.

Now, if a beneficent, omnipotent God exists, He could annihilate evil at will, and He could end all pain and suffering anytime He chooses. A being who has the power to do this would be cruel and unjust not to exercise it, and thus end all evil and its consequences, right? Here is the rub: if you are going to end all evil you must begin with evil wherever it may be. If God does this, then all of us are no longer here. All beings who have the power to choose have, within one thousandth of a second of His decree, ceased to exist. If the only way to deal with evil is to annihilate it as an actual and a potential, then you destroy its actual and potential manifestation. And the moment you do that, you have successfully annihilated the entire human race.

Do you see what you're really trying to do? In effect, you're saying to God, "If I had the power, I could do it better than You can." But if we were given the power, hypothetically, we just couldn't do it.

If we're going to deal with the problem of evil, let's deal with it from the perspective of God, not from the perspective of men. The solution to evil is not instantaneous annihilation. The solution from God's perspective is to work it all out for His own glory and for man's redemption. It is no accident that Romans 8:28 remains one of the foundations of divine revelation: "And we know that God causes all things to work together for good to those who love God, to those who are called according to *His* purpose" (NASB).

Scripture is telling us that God looks down on the evil which has come from free choice, and He says, "I will not intervene in it except to exercise My free choice, to cause the goals of evil to be turned to the ultimate glory of My purpose." God is not cruel and unjust. He is infinitely loving and patient, constantly and consistently working all things out for good.

Q: *Is it true that we live in a multi-dimensional reality?*

The Bible is a dimensional book in the sense that a dimension is a realm of reality, sometimes imperceptible, but nonetheless genuine. Human beings live in a dimension subject to the five senses, and they tend to make the mistake of believing that anything beyond the realm of those senses is simply not there. To accept such reasoning would be a fatal mistake from a biblical perspective.

Even as people live in the dimension of Earth, so the Bible says there is another dimension of heaven, where God reigns as Sovereign. This second dimension of heaven, or the throne of God Himself, is more real than human senses can perceive; it was a dimension that was bridged when God chose to become man in the Person of Jesus Christ. Because of Him, mankind now has access into a realm of infinite power, indescribable love, and cosmic justice.

The third dimension is one of spiritual darkness, controlled by Satan and his hosts.

Q: *Why does God send people to hell?*

God sends people where they choose to go. The Bible teaches that Jesus Christ came into the world to deliver men from this darkness, because originally hell was prepared not for man, but for Satan and his followers. They go there by divine decree, while man is the only creation that chooses it freely.

This is clearly derived from Jesus' words: "Then shall he say also unto them on the left hand, Depart from me, ye cursed, into everlasting fire, prepared for the devil and his angels" (Matt. 25:41). Whatever hell's dimension may be, one thing is absolutely certain: if it required the death of the most perfect Being who ever lived to deliver us from it, then it is to be avoided at all costs.

Q: *Who is Satan?*

According to Ezekiel 28:12–19, where he was addressed as the "king of Tyrus," he was once a beautiful, created being—a marvelous messenger of light. Satan's original name, "Lucifer" means "light-bearer," and he occupied a position of tremendous privilege and responsibility in the kingdom of heaven.

The prophet Isaiah tells us that Lucifer revolted against the throne of God because he wanted to be like the Most High God, thereby falling from his place of glory through his pride (Isa. 14:12–21). Jesus said that He beheld Satan falling from heaven like lightning (Luke 10:18), which, for Christians, removes all doubt of Satan's existence and fall.

He lost the radiance and splendor that reflected from the throne of the Lord, with which he was anointed because of his exalted position. Despite this, Lucifer (at this point, renamed Satan) threw the whole force of his own being and of his partners in angelic rebellion into a great cosmic war intended to disrupt God's divine plan and win for himself either terms of armistice with the Creator, or else ultimate triumph.

Q: *Why didn't Jesus kill the devil when He knew all the bad things Satan would do?*

The Bible says that in order to further His divine plan for the ages, God created freedom of choice. Without freedom of choice, love is not possible. God gave to angels and men the freedom to choose. God is responsible for creating the capacity of choice, but not responsible for the exercise of that choice against His will. The exercise of will against God is sin, and that is the origin of sin.

Lucifer was neutral, knowing no concept of evil, and he had the capacity to choose. Choosing his will brought judgment. God decided to use that judgment as a means of redeeming mankind, and that's exactly what He did.

God could annihilate the devil right now in 1/10,000th of a microsecond, but it would not fulfill the divine plan of the ages. So, we go through this because sin has entered the world, and death by sin. Christ is the answer to sin. Redemption is God's goal for the universe. We made our choice and Satan made his. Do not object to God making His choice. He said, "I'm going to use it for My glory, so that the wrath of men and angels will end in praise."

I don't know how that's going to happen, but I have a sneaking suspicion it's going to work out fine, and I'm willing to let Him do it in His own good time.

Q: *I have a buddy who collects unicorns. He doesn't make a habit of going out and looking for them, but he has a few of them, and he is wondering if they're linked to anything satanic.*

No, nothing satanic. In mythology, the unicorn is mentioned sometimes with occultic or supernatural connections; other times they're just a curiosity. But as far as being a symbol that can absolutely be traced to satanism, no.

There is a dangerous teaching loose in the church today. Many Christians have been victimized by it, and therefore it must be examined and thoroughly eliminated. The New Testament knows nothing of demon possession for Christians. It doesn't teach it.

First Corinthians 6:19 is clear: "Do you not know that your body is a temple of the Holy Spirit, who is in you, whom you have received from God? You are not your own" (NIV). If the Spirit of God dwells within us, and Jesus said He would abide with us forever, then I have to believe that the Christian is exempt from demon possession.

We are not exempt from demonic influence, though. Use whatever terms you like—oppression, fascination—I have half a dozen descriptors of what can take place because of fascination with evil and with Satanic power. But none of them is possession. Possession is demonization, where the individual does not have the capacity to deal with it any longer.

When a person is truly demonized, they are beyond any help whatsoever, except divine help. I know, because I've conducted enough exorcisms to know what demon possession is; it is a very terrible and evil experience to have to undergo. It does not happen to Christians.

I know people who say, "But I know an example of this. I remember seeing that." I've seen a lot of these things, too, but this is an experience that should be tested by the Scriptures—Scripture should not be interpreted by the experience. We are to test all experience by Scripture, not the reverse. So, until I see biblical evidence for demon possession of Christians, I'm not going to accept anyone's testimony on the subject. I ask people all the time to produce the evidence. They cannot.

Demonic oppression works in quite a number of ways. If you yield yourself and become the servant of sin (Romans 6), you become its slave. Demonic power can influence you if you have yielded yourself to sin. The way demonic oppression takes place is that you lose your interest in the study of the Scriptures, your desire to be a witness, and the yearning for fellowship with other members of the body of Christ. Your prayer life virtually disintegrates, and if the demons are really after you and you have yielded yourself to sin, they can interfere with your psychological profile, with your thinking processes, and pretty generally wreak havoc in your life.

When something like this happens to you, it does not always mean it's demonic oppression, but these are characteristics that can go along with it. If you are born again, you cannot be demon possessed, because the Holy Spirit lives inside of you. Your body becomes His temple. If the devil knocks on the door, the Holy Spirit answers—and it's no contest.

Q: ***I've been talking to brothers and sisters on the subject of Judas, and they say that he is going to hell, but I feel we really can't pass that kind of a judgment.***

Now, wait a minute. God said that the person who betrayed the Messiah would end up in hell. Jesus said, "None of you is lost, except the son of perdition; that the scripture might be fulfilled" (John 17:12). And he, Judas, was the son of perdition because he betrayed innocent blood, so he was lost.

Q: ***How can both Lucifer and Jesus be referred to in the same way? Isaiah 14:12 says, "How you have fallen from heaven, / O star of the morning, son of the dawn" (NASB). And then over in Second Peter 1:19 it says, "you do well to pay attention as to a lamp shining in a dark place, until the day dawns and the morning star rises in your hearts" (NASB).***

The phrase, "Lucifer, son of the morning" ("star of the morning, son of the dawn," NASB) refers to his condition before he fell. He was an angel of light, and the word *angel* means "messenger."

If you go to Peter, it's referring to Jesus Christ and to His second coming; when Christ returns, He will return as the Light of the World. So, He's spoken of as the "Daystar," or "morning star," or as the radiant light, because it's a reference to Him.

Lucifer was at very best a reflection of the glory of God, and as such was called the light-bearer. But when he fell, he ceased to be an angel of light. So, you can't take the context referring to Lucifer and transpose it to Peter, because they're two different contexts.

Q: ***What's your opinion on Halloween? I don't know whether I should back it up as a Christian or not.***

Halloween is connected with the world of the occult. About that there is no doubt and anyone that ignores it is being unrealistic. Now, the big question is, there are all kinds of things in our daily lives that are connected with paganism. The months of the year and the days of the week all have names derived from pagan sources, and we don't think much about that at all. There are pagan holidays that we've absorbed into the Christian calendar, and we don't spend much time dwelling on those.

Today, Halloween has largely become a cultural thing where kids go out trick or treating, and it's a fun time for the kids. I think that the influence of the occult on Halloween and through Halloween is probably negligible when it comes to trick or treating. However, people ought to be aware of the fact that Halloween's origin is occultic and anything that people try and emphasize connected with the occult at Halloween should be very definitely resisted and unmasked.

So the best thing to do is to let this be a matter between the individual parents and the Lord, and if the parents feel very strongly that this occultic origin of Halloween is going to influence the children, fine, let them restrain them.

Q: *What is the difference between the three words used for hell in the Bible*—**Sheol, Hades,** ***and*** **Gehenna?**

Sheol is a Hebrew word in the Old Testament that sometimes (in context) refers only to the grave itself or to the pit where the body was placed. The context points to the meaning of the passage.

Other times, it refers to the place of departed spirits—those who are waiting for the coming of the Messiah—and other times, it refers to actual punishment and torment because of sin. The context will tell you the meaning, the usage of the word.

Hades is the equivalent of *Sheol* in the New Testament, except it never refers to just the grave itself. In the New Testament, it always refers to the place of departed spirits. Dr. Barnhouse used to say in *Hades* or *Sheol* that there's east *Sheol* and west *Sheol*—east hell and west hell. East hell is where the Old Testament saints were waiting for the coming of the Messiah, and west hell is where the wicked were being tormented because they rejected what God said. East hell doesn't exist anymore, only west hell exists, and those who are there remain there because they have rejected the Word of the Lord.

Hades refers to the place of departed spirits, and *Gehenna* is a reference to the hell of fire. Literally, it is taken from the Valley of Hinnom on the side of Jerusalem where they sacrificed children to Molech and burned garbage in a great garbage dump. They set it all on fire, and it constantly burned and smoldered. It was filled with rodents, worms, and everything else, so it became a picture of decay, of hell, and of constantly smoldering corruption.

That's why Jesus Christ said (quoting Isaiah the prophet) that hell is where the fire never goes out. He pointed outside the walls of Jerusalem, where the worm does not die. He wasn't talking about immortal worms living in fire. He was talking about the fact that the worm was the symbol of corruption. So, Gehenna is a figure of the lake of fire and of final judgment. Sometimes it's used for "west hell," but most of the time for the lake of fire. Jesus said it is better to enter into life maimed than to be hurled into *Gehenna.*

Q: ***I had a friend about six years ago who had a bad LSD trip. I ran into him a couple of weeks ago and he said he was a Christian. We talked a while, and he started discussing Satan—saying that he loved him. He's been in and out of insane asylums. Is he possessed? He reads the Bible, and says the words change him, but his god commands him to do things.***

You have to take a case of possession on its own merits and examine it. I would say the person is obviously mentally disturbed. When any "god" commands you to do anything inconsistent with what the God of creation has told you to do, then you know where it's coming from—either a deranged mind or Satan. So just pray for the person, but I wouldn't have him around.

Q: ***What do you think about psychic healing?***

There is such a thing as psychic healing. There is such a thing as opening the body and removing organs that's been observed and even photographed. Experts watched it happen so I believe some of it is *bona fide*. It is satanic. It has nothing to do with God, because the people performing it are spiritists, who deny the foundations of the gospel.

Satan's been in the healing business for a long time. Antichrist is going to be in the healing business. So, I don't see why we should be upset about it. It's there. What we should do is not make the mistake of assuming that simply because a miracle takes place that it automatically means God's behind it. Satan is in the miracle business and has been for centuries.

Q: *What does God think of astrology?*

The only answer to that question is what God has said about astrology. In Isaiah 47:12–14, you hear His opinion.

> Stand fast now in your spells
> And in your many sorceries
> With which you have labored from your youth;
> Perhaps you will be able to profit,
> Perhaps you may cause trembling.
>
> You are wearied with your many counsels;
> Let now the astrologers,
> Those who prophesy by the stars,
> Those who predict by the new moons,
> Stand up and save you from what will come upon you.
>
> Behold, they have become like stubble,
> Fire burns them;
> They cannot deliver themselves from the power of the flame;
> There will be no coal to warm by,
> Nor a fire to sit before!

God speaks of the judgment that is to come upon the astrologers, whom He classifies as sorcerers, occultists, and as people who commit those abominations that He also mentioned in Deuteronomy 18.

In the book of Daniel, you'll find the astrologers right in the middle of the world of the occult. There is no such thing as good astrology unless you rewrite Holy Scripture. There's only astrology and it is not based upon the Word of God; in fact, it is quite contrary to it.

Q: *Do demons have actual teachings?*

Take a good, long look at First Timothy 4:1: "But the Spirit explicitly says that in later times some will fall away from the faith, paying attention to deceitful spirits and teachings of demons" (NASB). This should arrest the attention of every Christian who takes the New Testament seriously because with one stroke of his pen, under the inspiration of the Holy Spirit, the apostle informs us there is such a thing as the teachings of demons. There is something that originates with Satan—that represents itself as pure religion and as truth.

Q: *What is the teaching of demons?*

In Acts 16 we see how the doctrine of demons works, and how detailed and thorough it is. It is not a theologian's pipe dream; it is a New Testament revelation. The pity is that it's not preached on very often, primarily because it can get quite sticky. But we ought to face it. Nothing is ever solved by running from it, only by facing it in the power of Christ's resurrection.

In Acts 16 the apostle Paul was carrying on a glorious ministry of evangelism. As he was preaching and carrying on this wonderful ministry, it was inevitable that Satan would make his appearance, and he did. Now what type of appearance did he make?

> As we were going to the place of prayer, we were met by a slave girl who had a spirit of divination and brought her owners much gain by fortune-telling. (Acts 16:16, ESV)

"Fortune-telling" in the Greek is *python*. This whole idea goes back to an ancient Greek cult. They were worshippers of a demon god called Pithios, who appeared on Mt. Olympus in the form of a snake. This girl was the representative of this deity. Through her powers she brought much gain to the people who utilized her services. Now, if you notice very carefully here, she followed Paul and cried out saying, "These men are servants of the Most High God, who proclaim to you the way of salvation" (Acts 16:17, ESV).

Please note this first: Satan is very pious. Satan clothes all forms of devilry in the most pious terminology. He announces to the world that Paul is a servant of the Most High God, proclaiming "the way of salvation." In the Greek, it says "a way" of salvation—the definite article "the" is not there. Satan doesn't recommend Jesus Christ's gospel. What he was saying was that these are servants of the Most High God and they are showing a way of salvation.

He's doing the same thing today: Jesus is an aspect of the truth; He is a fragment of the life. But under no circumstances will Satan acknowledge Jesus is eternal God incarnate—the *only* way, the *only* truth, the *only* life. Never.

This young girl walking behind them was crying out, but she wasn't doing the talking; and when the spirit was cast out, her masters were not happy. The Holy Spirit is very bad for business among demons. You'll notice that He ruins business among demons all the time. This is why occultism fears the presence of the Spirit. They don't fear other spirits, but they fear Christians who are filled with the Holy Spirit. They want no part of Spirit-filled Christians. Why? Because Christians have power from God to overcome them.

Christ as "a way": that is the first plank in the platform of the doctrine of demons. Jesus as "a way," but not *the way*. The spiritists say He is the greatest medium. The Bahai say He is one of nine great world prophetic manifestations of deity. The Jehovah's Witnesses say He's a super-angel named Michael. The Mormons say He's one god in a pantheon of divinities. But the record of Scripture is that He is indeed the Lord God Jehovah Himself in human form—and this they cannot face. That is why when Paul turned around and said, "In the name of Jesus Christ I command you to come out of her," they came out because no power is capable of resisting the Lord Jesus.

Christ as "a way." That is the kingdom of the occult and of the cults. You will notice it when you run across it in the doctrine of demons. Ask questions, probe. Some people will say you're being obnoxious. No, you're just concerned, and you should be. The world in which we live is disintegrating because people are not concerned. The Church must be concerned—desperately concerned.

Q: Some Satanists argue that Satan is just an idea or cosmic evil, and not a real being. What do you think?

The New Testament teaches a personal satanic being. It teaches there are evil beings, or spirit beings that control individuals. They are capable of creating illness, mental and physical; they are capable of binding people; they are capable of creating all forms of symptoms in human life and that—unrecognized—they can wreak awful destruction.

Now, there are people who feel it's fashionable to ignore the fact that there's such a thing as demonology in the Bible or that there is such a thing as the genuine and the truly important study of demons in the Old and the New Testament. But anyone who has any knowledge of Occultism or the Kingdom of the Cults knows immediately how foolish this is.

Demons are *not* little individuals running around in red union suits with pitchforks! (The devil loves to see the world make these caricatures of himself, particularly on Halloween.) Demons are, instead, malignant beings who are simply other-dimensional. They live in a dimension other than ours, but they are capable of entering this dimension.

Scripture says there are other dimensions. The Bible tells us there is the dimension of heaven, the throne of God. Quite obviously, it is not here. The Lord Jesus Christ ascended through the heavenlies, through dimensions into the heaven of heavens, the throne of God.

Another dimension mentioned in Scripture is populated by Satan, the prince of darkness, the god of this age, and the ruler of this world. He is here and his representatives are here. The New Testament gives us graphic illustrations of their presence and their power. For us to come to grips with them, we must first recognize there is such a thing as the dimension of Satan and the existence of demons. The New Testament reveals it to us in Ephesians 6:12. So we know there is the visible heaven we can see here with the stars, planets, and galaxies; there is a dimension beyond this which is under the control of the prince of the power of the air (2:2); and beyond that dimension is the throne of God.

The Bible tells us that were it not for the direct intervention of God the Holy Spirit, the church would be overcome by the power of Satan (2 Thess. 2:6). But it is the Spirit that restrains right now. That is why John exalts in First John 4:4, "You, dear children, are from God and have overcome them, because the one who is in you is greater than the one who is in the world." We are protected by the person, presence, and power of the Holy Spirit.

What precise evidence do we have for demons in the New Testament? The best example I can cite is Jesus Christ. We know that when Christ encountered the demons early in his ministry, He dealt with them. They are fallen angels, fallen spirits who followed Lucifer in his rebellion against the throne of God. They worshipped him, not God. They are quite literally Satan's children. When Christ encountered them He dealt with them, and they confessed something about Him in Mark 5:7 (NASB): "What business do we have with each other, Jesus, Son of the Most High God?"

When Christ encountered them, He expelled them. When He encountered Satan, He did not encounter the corporate evil within man; He did not encounter a philosophic abstraction; He was not simply using personification to speak of evil. When Jesus encountered the devil, He had a dialogue with him. Now, either Christ was schizophrenic—which the New Testament flatly rejects, as do we—or He was speaking with another dimensional being. In His conversation with Satan, Satan revealed something: "Again, the devil took him to a very high mountain and showed Him all the kingdoms of the world and their glory. 'All this I will give you,' he said, 'if you will bow down and worship me'" (Matt. 4:8–9). This is what Satan desires: worship.

Now, there's not a demon behind every lamppost and under every seat, but it is very foolish to assume there are none at all. This is precisely what the World has assumed and why we are in the condition we are in right now. This great force is loose. We are busily trying to give it other names but we will not succeed.

They are here. They are real. They are powerful. If we ignore them, we do so at our own peril.

Q: *Why did Jesus destroy an innocent herdsman's pigs in Mark 5:1–17, and at the same time, give Satan the right to make a deal as to where the demons could go?*

Good question, let's hope the answer is equally good. Jesus did not destroy an innocent herdsman's pigs—the demons did. They asked if they could go into the herd of pigs, and Jesus said yes. He didn't send them down the steep incline into the water; the demons took them there. Jesus didn't destroy them. He simply sent them into the swine and the swine destroyed themselves with demonic assistance.

The herdsmen weren't innocent anyhow, because the Bible forbids them to keep pigs, and they were keeping pigs, so they weren't innocent. Therefore, Jesus was bad for business because He had a slaughterhouse of water and that's where they went, and they didn't get their profit from the slaughterhouse. That's why they were angry at Him and asked Him to leave their community. They did not like the fact that Jesus was bad for business.

Q: *When Christ sent the demons into the swine it was cruel because he caused them to get killed (Mark 5:1–20). What do you say about that?*

My response to that is the demons asked to be sent into the swine. Remember, under Mosaic law swine were unclean and forbidden, and the people that were keeping the herds were disobeying the law of God. So, the Lord let the demons go into the swine to punish the people who shouldn't have had the swine to begin with.

Q: *I was listening to you on the* Bible Answer Man *program, and you said that Jesus said Judas was from the devil. How could Judas be from the devil if he healed people in Jesus' name?*

Read Matthew 7. The false prophets can preach in Jesus' name, prophesy in Jesus' name, call him Lord, cast out demons in Jesus' name, and work miracles in Jesus' name because the power is in the name of Jesus, and they are abusing it. That's how they do it and that's how Judas did it.

Judas was a man who fell from grace. He didn't have to betray Christ, but Scripture tells us that he would betray Him because God knew what he was going to do. Judas didn't betray Christ because the Scripture prophesied it and forced him to do it, though. The Bible says that God, who is outside of time and space, knew in advance what Judas would do, and gave us that message in His Word. Judas had free choice and he exercised that choice.

7

Eternity

Eternity—where we will spend it and why—was (not surprisingly) a recurring theme in many of Dr. Martin's question-and-answer sessions.

Q: *How do you enter into the kingdom of God?*

Jesus said you must be born again. "If you confess with your mouth Jesus as Lord, and believe in your heart that God raised Him from the dead, you shall be saved" (Rom. 10:9). When you confess Him as Lord, you are confessing that He is the Word of God made flesh.

God became man. Jesus is Lord to the glory of God the Father. So, if you want to enter the kingdom of God, you must believe in the Lord Jesus Christ and you will be saved. You become part of the ongoing kingdom of God.

Q: *In John 15:16, Jesus says, "You did not choose me, but I chose you and appointed you to go and bear fruit—fruit that will last. Then the Father will give you whatever you ask in my name" (NIV). What does this mean?*

This is a tremendous statement of the sovereignty of God. "You did not choose me, but I chose you." The choice of God is obviously based upon certain qualifications and certain factors that are not known to us. God does not arbitrarily, in eternity, see all mankind and say, "Eeny, meeny, miny, moe, these are the ones to heaven will go," and the rest are going to hell. That is not the way the mind of God works. That is not divine sovereignty.

Divine sovereignty takes into consideration whatever events, actions, and choices man is somehow involved in. In other words, there is an interrelationship between the sovereign will of God and the freedom that He granted to His creation. He retains His sovereignty, man retains a degree of freedom that God wants to give, and there is no conflict between the two.

He never explained predestination, He never explained foreordination, and He never explained election or the relationship of free will to any of those. That is not explained anywhere in Scripture. It is always left in the area of the crucible of faith.

Jesus told His disciples that though they did not understand what He was doing at the time, they would understand afterward (after He had risen from the dead). The same principle applies to us. The wise Christian will wait until afterward (when we get to heaven), and not spend his or her time chasing their predestination posterior throughout their entire life. That's like a dog running around in circles after a can tied to its tail. You can run around in circles for the rest of your life trying to solve the riddle of predestination, but you will never solve it. I have been down that route myself.

God is saying in John 15:16, "All you have to know is this: You didn't choose me, I chose you." But there is some basis on which God made the choice. The fact that we don't understand the basis doesn't mean that we're robots; it doesn't mean that God is some kind of arbitrary ruler who decides whatever He wants to do and takes nothing into consideration. That is not the God of the Bible.

There is knowledge that resides only in the mind of God about how God chooses. All you and I need to do is rejoice that

He loved us, that He extended that love to us in Jesus Christ, and we responded to it. We did not respond just by our own will, but by an interrelationship between our will and His choice that no one has ever been able to untangle.

Q: ***Does the Bible have anything to say as to whether or not the whole world has been reached with the gospel? If it has not, can we be sure that Jesus will not return until it has?***

The whole world has not been reached by the gospel. There are more than 800 languages that have not heard the Word of God, and definitely the gospel is to be preached in all the world before the end of the age comes. The Scripture says that.

Of course, as Hal Lindsey pointed out, the Jews who will be on earth during the tribulation period—the Remnant—are going to be witnessing with supernatural power, and evangelism will take place at that time. At the end of this is the consummation of the age. If you take the pretribulation position, this is a very viable explanation for it. If you take the posttribulation position, then you recognize the gospel must first be preached all over the world before the consummation of the age.

I don't get into debates like this primarily because it generates a great deal more heat than it does light, and I think it's a waste of time. There are many different positions, and we should consider all positions before we make up our minds. We should be open-minded. Some people claim to be open-minded, and they always say they are willing to think about something, but as Dr. Barnhouse once pointed out, when people say they are going to think about something, it generally means they're rearranging their prejudices. He was pretty sharp in areas like this.

Q: *I have a question on predestination in the particular case of Judas Iscariot. It was prophesied that one would betray the Messiah, correct? Judas Iscariot happened to be that one. In a sense, doesn't it seem like he had no choice as the individual who betrayed Jesus?*

Be careful here, you're getting into double predestination. The Bible teaches predestination: God has selected from all eternity people who are going to live with Him—not because of their goodness, but because of His grace. That's an absolute, biblical teaching.

The basis on which God has made that choice has never been presented in Scripture. It rests wholly in the mind of God, so in order to understand predestination's ultimate meaning, one would have to understand the mind of God, and we do not have that privilege—that's point one.

Point two is this: the fact that God knows something is going to happen does not mean that God has fixed it to occur. I may know that my car is going to be in my garage tomorrow morning at 6 a.m., because I parked it there at 6 a.m., and I knew absolutely it will be there. That's the way I have to make something certain, but that doesn't mean God has to do it that way.

So, I couldn't possibly say that Judas Iscariot was predestined to damnation and therefore was not responsible for what he did. I'd have to say that Judas Iscariot had the option of not doing it, but God saw that he would.

Q: *Does Paul talk about an age of accountability?*

In Romans 7:9, Paul says, "I was once alive apart from the Law; but when the commandment came, sin became alive, and I died." It seems Paul's referring to a point when a child is at the age of accountability for their sin. That's the only possible interpretation of the passage in context.

Q: *If a child died before reaching this age of accountability, would the child be separated from God because of the original sin the child was born into?*

No, the whole point of Romans 7 is that there is a spiritual relationship with God that man has before the law touches that person's life. That's the whole argument that Paul is giving—I was alive. The (Greek) word is not *bios*. *Bios* is physical life; *Záō* is spiritual life. Paul is saying, "Once I was spiritually alive until the law touched me. When the law touched me, I died, which means I lost my relationship to God."

Paul is saying, "There was a time when I was alive." We enter the world under a suspended sentence of death because of Adam's sin, but God is just and gracious. He does not implement that justice in our lives until we follow Adam's pathway. When that happens, the judgment hits us. Up until that time we are not accountable, we are under grace.

Now that upsets a lot of people—but let them get upset with the apostle Paul. He said it, I didn't, and it's a very sound argument. Some of the church fathers were smart enough to catch on to that also, and be delivered from the idea that babies who die unbaptized go to hell. That's absolute nonsense! That has nothing whatever to do with Scripture. It is theology that evolved in the early church, and unfortunately it took hold and people began to believe it. Today, people still believe that you've got to get water on that baby or the baby's going to die and go to hell (or to limbo, in Catholic theology), and be separated from the beatific vision of the Person of God. But Jesus said, "It is not the will of your Father who is in heaven that one of these little ones should perish" (Matt. 18:14). That's good enough for me. I will leave it with the mercy of the Lord Jesus Christ.

Q: *Will we recognize our loved ones when we are raptured?*

Maybe some of them won't want to recognize you! Seriously, the Scripture says that we don't know what we will be like but we know that when Jesus appears, we shall be like Him, for "we shall see him as he is" (1 John 3:2). We're going to have a body like His own glorious body and John says, we shall know even as we are known (1 Cor. 13:12)—and that means you will know the person.

Just to speculate: I think it would be marvelous, and I know God can do a lot better than I think, but I thought of how it might be if we see a person we love but we see them differently than we knew them in the past. For instance, a grandfather. What if we could recognize a grandfather, but he looked young? Or what if God allows each of us to see someone as they looked when we loved them?

We may see other people differently at different stages. You may think, well, how could that be? I don't know, but with God nothing is impossible. If He wants to make everyone happy, why not have everyone see their loved ones at the ultimate moment of their greatest love and affection?

I don't know how God's going to do it, but I have ultimate confidence in His ability to make us happy. He says He's going to, and I'm going to trust Him for it.

Q: *Are we at the end of the ages? It seems like Second Timothy 3:1–5 is totally true today: "This know also, that in the last days perilous times shall come. For men shall be lovers of their own selves, covetous, boasters, proud, blasphemers, disobedient to parents, unthankful, unholy, Without natural affection, trucebreakers, false accusers, incontinent, fierce, despisers of those that are good, traitors,*

> ***heady, highminded, lovers of pleasures more than lovers of God; having a form of godliness, but denying the power thereof: from such turn away."***

This portion of Scripture is seldom preached because it upsets people, and I figure that any section of Scripture that upsets a number of people must be worthwhile, and must have a great deal to recommend it. The spirit of the age in which we live cannot be safely ignored by the Christian church. It is not an age which breathes kindness and tolerance, compassion, understanding or love. It is an age which brings out the very worst of the character of man.

We have been at the end of the ages, according to the apostle John, for almost two thousand years, and we are moving forward to the cosmic day of divine judgment. It is not unloving to tell people the truth. You can get into a great deal of trouble for doing it, but if you're in the ministry of God to win popularity contests, you have chosen the wrong place. You are supposed to be a witness for Jesus Christ no matter what it costs, under whatever circumstances face you.

Now, I want to tell you something that may make you unhappy—and after careful consideration, I really don't care! It's the truth. Today the church is under attack on multiple fronts by atheism, agnosticism, and skepticism. Secular humanism poisons the minds of our children so that we send them to school singing, "All Hail the Power of Jesus Name," and they come out spouting every kind of false doctrine and teaching imaginable. We have made the mistake of thinking that if we preach Jesus Christ, it is not necessary to defend his gospel. Let me tell you something: it is a command to defend the gospel of Christ. It is necessary to defend the gospel of Christ.

You must see the nature of the enemies of the gospel: they can look like us, they can sound like us, they can purr like pussycats, they can quote our Bible, but when we get down to the rock-bottom truth of Jesus Christ, they will not believe in Him. They will oppose the gospel, and they will destroy the flock of God if you do not resist them in Jesus' name.

Q: *When we are raptured, will the Lord change those who are alive first or is it the dead in Christ who will rise first? Wouldn't the dead in Christ already be with the Lord?*

Yes, there's no doubt the dead in Christ will rise first and yes, First Thessalonians 4 tells us they are with the Lord. You will also find confirmation for this in Second Corinthians 5 and Philippians 1. The immaterial nature, the spirit or the soul of the believer is in the presence of the Lord. About that, there can't be any doubt at all.

What First Thessalonians 4 is saying is that God is going to bring back with him those spirits, those souls, and they will be instantly reunited with their resurrection body. They will be created in the twinkling of an eye. As fast as you can blink your eye, the resurrection body will be immediately joined with the descending spirits so they'll be clothed with immortality as they come back to earth with Christ.

Q: *But what would the Lord want with bodies that were already dead and decomposed?*

He wouldn't want the bodies in the grave that are dust—bodies that were eaten by fish or incinerated by fire. First Corinthians 15 says you are not getting those bodies back. The resurrection body is created by God instantaneously at the second advent of Jesus Christ.

When Scripture talks about the dead in Christ rising first, it is not talking about the body in the grave, but about an instantaneous change in which the resurrection body is instantly united with the spirit. That will take place faster than you can blink your eye. One sure thing in this crazy world is the word of Christ.

Q: *In Revelation 13 where it speaks about the beast—will it be the Antichrist?*

The beast that rises out of the nations—out of the sea—the sea is a symbol for the nations. It is considered to be the Antichrist because it is the number of a man that he possesses. "Here is wisdom. Let him who has understanding calculate the number of the beast: for the number is that of a man; and his number is six hundred and sixty-six" (Rev. 13:18, NASB). So, the beast is identified as a man, and this has classically been interpreted as the Antichrist.

Q: *Revelation 13:3 says, "And I saw one of his heads as it were wounded to death; and his deadly wound was healed: and all the world wondered after the beast." Is this the Antichrist he's speaking about that was wounded? Does this mean a man is going to be wounded in the head and his wound is actually going to be healed up?*

"I saw a beast coming up out of the sea, having ten horns and seven heads. And ten diadems on his head were blasphemous names. And the beast, which I saw was like a leopard" (Rev. 13:1). This is symbolic language, descriptive of satanic power, and it ends up personified in the man of sin—the Antichrist.

The wound is open to debate. There are theologians who take it literally, some who take it figuratively, and some that take it historically. A few theologians have even interpreted this to be the papacy. I've read the theologians and the commentaries on this. The historical interpretation has some things in it that appeal to me because I love history. The figurative has appeal to me because a lot of the Book of Revelation is figurative, but I honestly do not know all of the meaning of the symbols that are used here.

I can tell you this much, though, the Antichrist is a single person. The Antichrist will be identified by the number 666, and the Antichrist is described in Second Thessalonians 2 as the man of sin who opposes and exalts himself above all that is called deity. He will sit in the temple of God proclaiming that he is God, and then the Lord Jesus will utterly ruin him with the outshining brightness of His glorious second coming. I believe that implicitly. That's a general outline of Antichrist in the New Testament.

Q: *I know God has forgiven my sins because of Jesus, but sometimes I feel so condemned when I remember the things I've done. What's your advice for me?*

If you go through the commands of God, you will see how all of them are consummated in love. Love is not some sticky, gooey emotional substance cooked up by theologians as an excuse for doing almost anything. God expressed love in Jesus Christ. This is the ultimate expression of love: "Love one another as I have loved you" (John 13:34).

We should not condemn ourselves for past sins—we are clean in the sight of God when we've asked for forgiveness and changed how we live our lives. The law of God cannot touch the Christian because the Christian has already died in Jesus Christ and risen again. We are not under the law—we are under grace. God's rule of the spirit of life through Christ Jesus (Romans 8:1).

I wonder if we recognize exactly what's happened? God is saying to us, "I will not hold you before My throne for eternal judgment. I will not charge your sins to your account. I have already charged them to Jesus of Nazareth, and I have given you My Spirit so that you may walk with Me in the light," having fellowship with each other in the blood of Jesus Christ, that goes right on cleansing us every day from sin (1 John 1:7).

If we love each other as Jesus loved us, we will have no difficulty fulfilling the righteousness of the law. We will be fulfilling everything that God demands if we are loving Him and our neighbor as ourselves. The law of the spirit of life in Christ Jesus is the law of love, and it has set us free from sin and death.

Q: *Isn't there some passage in the Bible that indicates pets live on after death?*

There is no evidence in the Bible that pets live on—man is a living soul, animals are not. I know some psychic researchers today teach that animals live on, but I don't accept psychic evidence. It does not come from God, but from the devil. So, I would have to say that if someone told me that Fido was barking on after death and going on about his business, or that Tabby was meowing in the great hereafter or in that great cathouse in the sky, I think at that particular juncture I'd have to blow it away by saying that God deals with human souls. Christ died for the sins of men and not for the perpetuity of the animals.

Q: *Paul says to be absent from the body is to be at home with the Lord. He also says we will be rewarded in heaven according to our works. What will our relationship be with God between the day we die and Judgment Day?*

All I can tell you is in Philippians 1, Paul said he was looking forward to that relationship—that to die and be with Christ was a lot better than staying here. As I look at the world around me, and the progressive disintegration of my body and everyone else's, I am confident of the fact that things have got to be better with Christ.

Don't ask me what's going to go on there because I don't know, but I do know this—joy and happiness is where Jesus is, and I am looking forward to that eternal joy and happiness. I will relish it all the more because I know that I'm not worthy of it. It is by grace that God has saved me and you, and that's enough to give us all a nice warm feeling for all eternity. Salvation is a gift.

Q: *What about the signs of the times and the imminent appearing of Christ?*

Well, if we're discussing my personal conviction, it's possible that Christ may not come back for another thousand years. So I'm just saying, be careful trying to set brackets for the return of Christ. I think that could be dangerous. You don't know when the Lord is coming back. I think you have to live in terms of biblical prophecy.

Q: *What do you think about all the arguments about the return of Christ?*

A great evangelist of the past once said that churches by and large have become places where we have soft lights, soft music, and even softer sermons, and as a result people have been lulled into a false sense of security. I think we have to come to grips with the fact that the end of the ages which the Christian church must face is upon us. It is to be a time of great trouble and trial for Christianity.

Now, I am certainly not going to argue about the pretribulation, midtribulation, or posttribulation positions, or whether Jesus is coming before the tribulation, in the middle of the tribulation, or after the tribulation. I have a dear friend who says he's a "pan-tribulationist": everything is going to pan out in the end. I think he's probably closer to the truth than he knows.

We've been so busy fighting among ourselves. We are so busy arguing about whether or not Christ is going to come before the tribulation, in the middle of the tribulation, or after the tribulation—which is pure tribulation, anyhow! Premillennial, amillennial, postmillennial; sprinkle 'em, pour 'em, or immerse 'em. Give them wine, grape juice, or Coca-Cola at the Communion service, with leavened bread or unleavened bread. Bishops, ruling elders, and deacons; no bishops, no ruling elders, no deacons. Back and forth, in and out, up and down—the whole world is going to hell on the doorstep while we're fighting about nothing!

We must get our minds off peripheral theology and get down to the main business of the church, which happens to be how to reach the world. There are many people awaiting the second advent of Jesus Christ who do nothing for the Kingdom. They're so heavenly-minded they're no earthly good, and this is exactly what we want to avoid.

Q: *What is "the day of the Lord?"*

Fantastic as it may seem, the prophetic theology of both the Old and New Testaments concerning the Messiah of Israel describes a Savior who first suffers for the sins of the world and then, because of his rejection by the world, returns to judge it. The hope of the ages, then, is the return of Jesus Christ—no longer the sin-bearer and object of contempt and rejection by sinful and unappreciative men, but now the Sovereign Judge of the cosmos, whose glorious appearance will trigger the events known in Christian theology as "the day of the Lord."

> But the day of the Lord will come like a thief. Then with a tremendous crash the heavens will pass away; the burning elements will be dissolved; the earth too and the works in it shall be burned up. Since all these things are thus to be dissolved, how consecrated and reverent your behavior should be, as you are expecting and hastening on the coming day of God, on whose account the blazing heavens will be dissolved and the burning elements melted. But we are, in agreement with His promise, looking for new heavens and a new earth in which righteousness is at home. (2 Pet. 3:10–13, MLB)

Q: ***A friend gave me a book called* Bible Readings for the Home, *and it teaches that the millennium will be spent in heaven and not on the earth. I have a problem with that. They say the word rendered "bottomless pits" in the text is "abysses" and that for those thousand years, the earth is going to be uninhabited.***

That is a Seventh-day Adventist publication, and it doesn't follow logically or theologically. Here's why: simply because the word describing a chaotic earth is translated "abyss" in the Septuagint in Genesis, doesn't mean that Revelation is referring to a chaotic earth. It's referring to a place of chaos which is designated as the bottomless pit where Satan is going to be restrained, along with his demonic forces, for a period of 1,000 years. The Adventists don't accept this, though, so we have a difference of opinion.

You can do all kinds of word studies to try and connect passages, but you're not going to be able to do it unless the contexts are the same, and they don't have the same context in Revelation as they do in Genesis.

Incidentally, this view did not originate with the Adventists. It was held by Christians for a long time before the Adventists ever appeared on the scene. There are a number of views about the millennium in different schools of interpretation of the book of Revelation. I would recommend a very good book for you: *Revelation: An Expositional Commentary* by Donald Grey Barnhouse (Grand Rapids: Zondervan, 1971).

Q: ***If Adam and Eve hadn't fallen and we as their children live in a perfect earth, would we have lived here eternally? Isn't it better to die as we do and go to heaven?***

Do you mean that you want to improve on God's ideas in the beginning? No, it wouldn't be. We don't know what God had in store for an unfallen creation, but we know what He has in store for a restored creation: a new heaven and a new earth, wherein dwells righteousness. We'll be citizens of both places, heaven and earth. Right now, we're only citizens of heaven. Did you know that? You are not a citizen of earth if you are born again. Your citizenship is in heaven, where you're looking for the Lord Jesus. We are strangers and pilgrims here, thank God.

Q: ***First Thessalonians 4:16–17 says, "the dead in Christ shall rise first." If we go to be with the Lord at the rapture, everyone in Christ receives a new body. So who are the dead in Christ?***

Those who have physically died believing in Jesus Christ are called the dead in Christ. They are alive in the Spirit. Their bodies will rise first out of ashes or from the sea. The Scripture says God will give a body as it pleases Him, and your new body will not have one atom of your old one in it. That's right, it's a new creation in the image of the Lord Jesus Christ. So, I wouldn't get too upset about it, I can't wait to get mine. This one is beginning to wear out on an accelerated scale.

Q: ***In Luke 23:43, Jesus said to the thief on the cross, "Truly I tell you, today you shall be with Me in paradise." Is paradise the same as heaven?***

It is now, but up until then, it was the place of departed spirits, "Abraham's bosom" (Luke 16:22), where people waited for the coming of the Messiah.

Q: ***When do you believe the rapture will take place?***

It will take place at the end of the tribulation period, in accordance with Second Thessalonians 1. The Lord Jesus shall descend for the church in flaming fire, to judge the world. That has been the historic position of the Christian church for 1900 years, before the

Plymouth Brethren arrived and Hal Lindsey popularized the pre-tribulation rapture. That position is not a classical biblical position.

Q: ***Does it say anywhere in the Bible that when we go to heaven, we will actually recognize each other?***

Yes, it does. Paul says we shall see face to face, and know even as we are known (1 Cor. 13:12). We will understand each other just as we do now—for which we can praise the Lord.

Q: ***If all my family and I go to heaven, will we be together there? With my husband and children?***

If they're born again, you will—absolutely. I don't know of any segregated quarters in heaven, so unless you just personally don't like them, you will be together.

If you don't like them, I would pray for grace because you're going to have to get along with them there, so you might as well start now.

Q: ***Revelation 6:10 says that those in heaven cried out to the Lord, asking Him how long before He did something about those who martyred them. I thought there were no feelings of vindictiveness in heaven?***

It doesn't say they are vindictive. It says that they are crying out to God for justice, and that's what they're going to get, because God says He will avenge His own. This means He will give perfect justice to those who have persecuted His children. This comes at the end of the ages after the persecution of the Antichrist. God will then swiftly bring justice.

Q: ***Can you recommend a good book which explains the end-time prophecies?***

There are many books which explain the end-time prophecies. *Things to Come* (Zondervan, 1964) is a very good one by

J. Dwight Pentecost of Dallas Theological Seminary. I don't agree with Dr. Pentecost on the tribulation period, but he is a very faithful biblical scholar. He's done a fine job of putting a great deal of this material together. A posttribulation book on the subject is *The Church and the Tribulation* by Robert Gundry (Zondervan, 1973). George Ladd's *The Blessed Hope and Crucial Questions Concerning the Kingdom of God* (Eerdmans, 1956) is also excellent. There are many others, such as Alexander Reese's *The Approaching Advent of Christ* (Marshall, Morgan & Scott, 1937), but those are just a few for you to get going on.

Q: ***Do you believe that the land and water areas of the earth will be the same during the Millennium as now? Also, will the nations, cities, landmarks, roads and such conveniences as planes, TV, radio will be here when Christ rules the earth? Hal Lindsey says that thermonuclear destruction will be so great during the tribulation that the earth will need to be refurbished and the curse removed. Do you agree?***

If there is a thermonuclear war, he is right. If there is not, there is no need for it. But since he doesn't know and I don't know, we are only sharing the abundance of our ignorance if we guess. The smartest thing to say is that the Lord knows how the millennium is going to go and what it's going to be like, and I'm perfectly content to leave that in His hands—primarily because I've got enough trouble with a cursed earth now without dealing with a judged earth then. So, I don't know and I don't think Hal knows either, but people are given to speculation and I think that kind of speculation sometimes leads people on the wrong path.

8

Miscellaneous Questions

Often Dr. Martin's audiences, whether at his speaking events or on his radio program, asked questions that did not fall neatly into a specific category, or sought his opinion on issues that the Bible does not directly address. In these cases, Dr. Martin gave his honest opinion and tried, when possible, to cite the counsel of Scripture.

Q: *What makes life tolerable? What banishes the fear of death?*

It's not doctrinal or philosophical theology, not prophetic interpretation, and not the doctrine of the Second Advent. What banishes the fear of death is the person of the risen Christ. Because Jesus Christ is alive, all the philosophical, logical, and religious arguments against Christianity disintegrate. Because He lives, all the arguments of the world are nonsense. Because He came out of the tomb immortal, death will be swallowed up by life.

Do you know, you can't talk about Christmas without celebrating the Resurrection? When you're talking about the baby who came into the world by God the Holy Spirit, you've got to talk about the man who was raised from the dead by God the Holy Spirit.

I'll tell you something: I'm going to be so glad to trade in this carcass for that immortal body! I'm going to be so glad to enter at last into the presence of peace that knows no description, joy that is inexpressible, and victory that is ours by grace. The Christian can rejoice in Jesus Christ because He is a living Savior. Buddha,

Mohammed, Confucius, Zoroaster, and all the philosophers of earth share one common factor—they're all dead! There isn't one of them that made it back. But Jesus Christ's gospel was propelled for almost two thousand years by one fact—He lives!

The empirical and scientific proof that He lives is the fact that He transforms the lives of people: He takes the drug addict, the prostitute, the disgruntled, and the downtrodden; He takes the proud and the arrogant; He takes what you are and where you are, and with the touch of divine grace, He transforms you and recreates you. There are no retreads with God—only re-creations.

The acid test of Christianity was not the prophecies of the Old Testament, nor was it the forensic debating capacities of the apostles. It was not the good life that was led, or even the miracles that were performed. The acid test of Christianity is whether or not Jesus Christ could conquer death. Every living person knows they must die. The death rate is still one per person. You're going to die and I'm going to die if Jesus Christ does not come back in our lifetime.

What banishes the fear of death? What makes life tolerable? The person of the living Christ. He is alive, and He conquered death!

Q: *Do we know where Simon Peter is buried?*

They found Peter's tomb in Rome a few years ago, and it's been identified. It specifies on the tomb, "This is Simon Peter."

Q: *If salvation is unconditional, then wouldn't requiring someone to speak in tongues be a condition?*

There's only one condition for redemption: believe in the Lord Jesus Christ, and you will be saved.

Q: *Does Scripture support capital punishment?*

Yes, it does. God said this before the Ten Commandments were given and never changed it. "Whoever will shed the blood of man by man shall his blood be shed" (Gen. 9:6). Premeditated murder is to be rewarded with execution. That is the law that God brought to bear on mankind. The bleeding hearts that don't want any part of it are the people who feel sorry for the Hillside Strangler and others like him, rather than for the victims that monster destroyed.

Q: *Does God hear the prayers of unbelievers?*

If you're an unbeliever, there are unforgiven sins in your heart and God says He does not answer your prayers because you don't have a right to a relationship with Him (Isa. 59:2). God hears all prayers, though. God answers all prayers, but He says no to the prayers that ignore Jesus Christ (James 1:6–7).

If your prayers can be answered apart from the Son of God, tell me, what was the purpose of the cross? What is the purpose of the resurrection? What is the purpose of the gospel? If you're going to get there by worshipping Vishnu or Kali or praying to Buddha's statue, or by deliberately rejecting Him as your Messiah, then the whole Christian gospel becomes a charade and a joke.

People may say that's very arbitrary that God only answers certain prayers, but Jesus told us to pray believing (Mark 11:24) and that's how we know He answers the prayers of believers, those who trust Him. I know He answers the prayers of unbelievers—He says no—except for the prayers of unbelievers that cry out for salvation. He says yes to them.

Some people say, well, that's very narrow. Jesus said, "Strait is the gate, and narrow is the way, which leadeth unto life, and few there be that find it (Matt. 7:14). Why? They are all looking for the broad path. God says it's this way. There's a big road over there, but it's not the super-highway. You may argue with your Creator about this, but He is the One who makes the rules. Does that register with you? You are breathing His air right now. Your life is not your own. All He has to say at any given moment is "Pfft!"—and that is the last we will hear from you.

I had to laugh at the atheist I used to debate over and over again in New York. He was arguing about God not being here, and I told him it's very unsafe to discuss the existence of your Creator in His presence. He didn't like that.

Robert Ingersoll, a famous agnostic, used stand up in his public speeches, take a watch out, put it on the table and say, "If there's a God in heaven, I give Him three minutes to strike me dead!" Everyone waited and nothing happened.

One time he pulled that same stunt on a bishop he was debating. When he got finished, he turned to the bishop and said, "I'm still alive." The bishop said to him, "Do you really think the patience of God Almighty can be exhausted by someone like you?"

Ingersoll had no response to that.

I keep telling people—as a warning, not a threat—that it's very unsafe to play games with God. It's very dangerous because you never know when the Lord will say to you what He said to the children of Israel. Remember, they were griping all the time about the things that were happening to them: "Would to God we were back in Egypt, would to God we had food, would to God we were dead in the desert"—would to God this, would to God that. The most chilling verse in the Book of Numbers is this one: "You have wept [in complaint] in the ears of the LORD. . . . Therefore the LORD will give you" (Num. 11:18).

Think that over; if you follow that road you may end up saying, "I'm sorry I was ever born!" And sadly, there may be people who agree with you. Did you ever think of that? But you're here and this is His universe. People seem to forget. He made it, it's His. You live in His ballpark and play by His rules. So many say, "I don't want to do that," and in the end, He'll take care of that, too.

Q: *What is a good reference book on the different Christian denominations?*

Frank Mead, *Handbook of Denominations in the United States* (Abingdon, 1949), or Elmer T. Clark, *Small Sects in America* (Abingdon, 1995).

Q: *I've been talking to some people who seem to believe there's a worldwide reformation or renewal in the Catholic church. Is it possible for a born-again Christian to remain in the Catholic church system and still be saved?*

I think there are born-again people in the Catholic church right now, witnessing for Christ in the Catholic Charismatic movement, and some of them have had a real reawakening to the Scriptures and to the ministry of the Holy Spirit.

God is at work universally in the Roman Catholic Church. It isn't what we would call a sweeping inferno, but there's definitely a brush fire. We should thank God for that, and I think we should work hard at spelling out the differences between orthodox Christianity and Catholicism, but not to the place where we alienate Roman Catholics, many of whom now know the Lord.

Q: *My Catholic roommate says that Matthew 18:34 sounds an awful lot like purgatory. What do you think?*

No, it doesn't sound like that at all. Jesus used this as an illustration. "So likewise will my heavenly Father do unto you." He's talking to the Jews. The context is Christ preaching to the Jewish constituency. "My heavenly Father will also do the same to you, if each of you does not forgive his brother from your heart" (18:35). He's enunciating the principle of the Lord's Prayer: "Forgive us our debts, as we forgive our debtors" (6:12). Jesus said if you don't do that, you're not a believer. So purgatory does not enter into the picture.

Q: *What happened to the fish in Noah's flood?*

The fish had to be exempted from the flood because water was their natural habitat, so whatever could survive in the water survived, and that could include crocodiles, lizards, and all kinds of fish.

Q: *Do you think the Seventh-day Adventists are some kind of a cult?*

It is not a non-Christian cult. It is a Christian sect or denomination with doctrines that, in certain places, are at variance with the Bible. A cult is a group of people gathered around someone else's interpretation of the Bible, but they deny the Trinity, the deity of Jesus, the virgin birth, the resurrection, and other key Christian doctrines.

Q: *I have a brother-in-law who is a believer, and recently he's been talking to somebody at his work who has convinced him that the only way to salvation is through predestination. Some days he's a Calvinist and some days he's an Arminian. Can you give me an idea what to say to him?*

All I can say is that the Bible teaches that from all eternity, God knew who was going to be saved. About that there is absolutely no doubt. Romans 8 says, "For whom He did foreknow, He did predestine to be conformed to the image of his Son." And it goes on to talk about the things that God did: election and predestination. All of these things are described in Scripture.

But the concept of predestination does not do away with free will. No one has ever been able to figure out, in the context of Scripture, where predestination and free will met in the mind of God when it came to knowing things in advance, and ordaining things to take place. No one has ever figured it out.

The confusion comes in when people start to think that if God predestines everything that He knows ahead of time, then He must have predestined evil. Surely He knew that Lucifer was going to fall, right?

Well, if He knew Lucifer was going to fall, and if He ordained him to fall because He knew it, then how can you hold Lucifer responsible for falling? You see, you get yourself backed into a corner and you're not going to get out easily. So that's why it's an involved subject.

Q: ***It sometimes feels as if good Bible teaching is a lost art. Do you agree?***

Yes, I think it is a lost art in some areas, but when you get into what God is trying to teach you, if you have any mind at all and any perception, you begin to sense that the Holy Spirit is tapping you on the shoulder and saying to you, "Here . . . here . . . here." Here is the answer to what you've been asking. Here is something that can help your life. Here is power and forgiveness, and it's all been provided for you by the God who ordains all things, and purposes all things after the counsel of his own will.

Q: ***Is the ark up in heaven? Does it say that in Hebrews?***

The real Ark of the Covenant is in heaven because the writer of Hebrews describes the ark as being in heaven. In Hebrews 8:5, we are told that the Ark of the Covenant here on earth was a copy of the real one in heaven.

Q: ***Do you feel that friction between the conservative dispensationalists and the liberal charismatics will cause a schism in God's church?***

I don't think you can ever have a successful schism in God's church because the Scripture says that the gates of hell will not prevail against the church. That means that the meanness and pettiness of men will not prevail against the church either. There are dispensationalists who are vigorously anti-charismatic, and there are some charismatics who at times get vigorously anti-dispensational. That will not alter the fact that both are members of the body of Christ, and that the Spirit will work in both of them as they are willing to yield to him.

I don't worry too much about splits of that nature. I rather say that the Lord will work out the details of it; all we have to do is be faithful where we are and let him take care of all of the rest of the things. It's when we start getting in the picture and mucking it up that things get confused and schismatic in the church.

There are genuine schisms or more serious division in the church. Paul says there has to be at some point so that the truth might be known. There must be arguments and divisions among you—partings of different opinions—he says in Corinthians, so that the truth may come out. What a terrible church it would be if everyone dressed the same, talked the same, decorated their houses the same, or had the same vocabulary all the time. It would be nauseating within a short period of time.

Look at the infinite variety—just in your church—that God in his mercy has been pleased to create. We are living proof that He has a sense of humor! People sometimes say to me, "Why do you mix humor with theology?" Because it needs it. In the midst of this cosmic zoo in which we live, you have to be able to laugh.

Q: *What do you think about a cosmic master in the New Age Movement who said they found many open minds in Los Angeles—exactly what the cosmic masters hoped to find?*

That's why they had their convention in Los Angeles; the open minds in Los Angeles were vacuum heads. There is a difference between being open-minded and having an empty head, you see. When you open your mind to the "cosmic masters" you are a vacuum head, because you are opening your mind to the doctrines of demons.

Q: *I would like your opinion on nuclear disarmament.*

I'm for it. I think it would be wonderful if we and the Russians and whoever else had them would agree to detonate them tomorrow in outer space, and just shoot them all out there and have done with it. Unfortunately, the people who are screaming for freezes and disarmament overlook a very important lesson of history: those who trust tyrants become their slaves.

Yuri Andropov was a tyrant. As a former head of the KGB, his hands were so red with the blood of innocent victims that I would personally not shake his hand. He was an evil man. President Reagan was absolutely correct; communism is an evil system. I'm sorry that the liberal press doesn't like that. I'm sorry that a lot of people criticized the president because of a strong moral stand on communism, but to trust the dictators with nuclear weapons or in a freeze where they have any advantage is to invite classic disaster. We dare not do this.

I would happily pay twice the taxes despite the waste of the Pentagon if it will prevent tyrants such as the Soviets ever thinking that there is a chance that they might overpower the United States. You are dealing with a very dangerous subject. You're dealing with human life on a massive scale.

I'll tell you what I'd like to do. I'd like to transport all the nuclear freeze people from the United States to the Soviet Union and have them picket there! Then they would understand what it means to be free. We should tolerate them; that's our Constitution. But listen to them? Not unless you have scrambled all your eggs, baby.

Q: *What do you think of fundamentalist end times survivalists who sequester themselves with arms and food, and wait for Armageddon?*

I think they have a long wait.

Q: *Aren't we Christians to take steps toward future famine or should we trust in the Lord's providence?*

Yes, we should take steps to prepare when there are indications that famine or danger is coming, and there will be plenty of indications. As to trusting in the Lord's providence—trust in the Lord with all thine heart and keep thy ammunition and food dry.

Q: *Does God ever allow us to see the future?*

The person who wants to interpret the future apart from God is a person who would lead you away from the Lord your God. What does Satan first try to do with his "seducing spirits, and doctrines of devils" (1 Tim. 4:1)? He tries to portray Jesus as *a way*, but not *the way*. Second, he tries to get people absorbed with the future. That is the second plank in this doctrine. Look at Acts 16. What was this girl involved in? Soothsaying. Do you know what a soothsayer is? Someone who predicts the future.

That person is dangerous, no matter who they are, even if they wear a cross around their neck. Crosses are cheap, and pious talk is cheap. What really counts is whether or not you have any substance to faith and reality to experience; whether or not you have been to the cross, and have been touched by the hand of the Lord Jesus. It is possible to be in the church, be baptized, teach Sunday School, be married to a Christian, and live it all out in the open—and still be filled with every kind of unclean spirit, if you have never been to the cross. There are people like this in our churches and all around us, and we wonder why the church is powerless. Why? Because Christians have no discernment.

Is it any wonder that Scripture tells us in First Corinthians 12 that one of the spiritual gifts is "discerning of spirits" (12:10)? We must be able to tell what we're dealing with, and God has not left us in darkness. I cannot help but think of Genesis 40 in this connection. Joseph, who was a prophet of God, was given this illumination by the Holy Spirit. This is what God has to say on the subject: "Do not interpretations belong to God?" (Gen. 40:8).

The only reliable source of information on the future is the Word of God. Any attempt to gain information from any other source is not only dangerous, but in direct contradiction to the teaching of Scripture. The future belongs to God. Don't play with it.

Q: *Is Communism a cult?*

No, it's not—not in the definition of a biblical concept of a cult. It's a form of political philosophy, and Karl Marx organized it. Most people don't know this, but he did. He organized it around the concept of the early Christian church. The Communist cell was the early Christians, according to Marx. He even wrote a defense of the deity of Christ, and professed to be a believer, before he apostatized with his book, *Das Kapital.* You have Marx imitating Christianity, and the Communists imitating the system of Christianity as a group of people who held things in common, but they are not a non-Christian cult. They are an alien philosophy.

Scripture Index

CLC
PUBLICATIONS
Fort Washington, PA 19034

This book is published by CLC Publications, an outreach of CLC Ministries International. The purpose of CLC is to make evangelical Christian literature available to all nations so that people may come to faith and maturity in the Lord Jesus Christ. We hope this book has been life changing and has enriched your walk with God through the work of the Holy Spirit. If you would like to know more about CLC, we invite you to visit our website:
www.clcusa.org

To know more about the remarkable story of the founding of CLC International we encourage you to read

LEAP OF FAITH

Norman Grubb

Paperback
Size $5\frac{1}{4}$ x 8, Pages 248
ISBN: 978-0-87508-650-7
ISBN (*e-book*): 978-1-61958-055-8

ESSENTIAL CHRISTIANITY

Walter Martin

Published originally in the 1970s, *Essential Christianity* is a readable explanation of the most important Christian teachings, with answers to such vital questions as:

- Is the Bible completely true?
- How can God be three in one?
- Is Christ really God and man?
- Who will be saved in the end?

. . .. plus dozens more crucially important questions about God, man and the universe. Essential Christianity will give you the answers you need in our confusing world of cults, half-truths, and religious confusion.

Paperback
Size 5 1/4 x 8, Pages 137
ISBN: 978-1-61958-344-3
ISBN (*e-book*): 978-1-61958-345-0